dear Auntie Betty

Happy Christmas 1991

with love,

Ingalo
x

The
Edinburgh
Book
of
Quotations

Illustrated by numerous Engravings.

Compiled by
Michael T. R. B. Turnbull

First published 1991
by B+W Publishing
Edinburgh
Printed in Scotland
at Meigle Printers
Galashiels
This selection
© Michael T.R.B. Turnbull
ISBN 0 9515151 6 0

Other B+W titles available

Edinburgh Walks Vol. 1
ISBN 0 9515151 0 1
Edinburgh Walks Vol. 2
ISBN 0 9515151 3 6
Glasgow Walks
ISBN 0 9515151 1 X
The Green Guide to Edinburgh
ISBN 0 9515151 5 2

Contents

Foreword by Neville Garden

The publishers would like to
thank The National Gallery
of Scotland for permission to
reproduce George Manson's
watercolour of the Cowgate.

ACKNOWLEDGEMENTS

My thanks to all the following for allowing quotations to be used:

Andrew Greig - extract from poem *Portobello Beach* (Surviving Passages. Canongate 1982); **Michael Grieve** - extracts from Hugh MacDiarmid's work (Edinburgh from *Lucky Poet* 1943); **Professor A J Youngson** - passage on Ann Street (*The Making of Classical Edinburgh 1750-1840*, EUP 1966); **Terry Quinn**, Editor, *Edinburgh Evening News* (Festivals section); **Magnus Linklater**, Editor, *The Scotsman* (Festivals section); **Magnus Linklater** - extracts from the works of Eric Linklater 1960; **Norman MacCaig** extracts from *Collected Poems* 1990; **Hazel Goodsir Smith** - extract from *Spring in the Botanic Garden* by Sydney Goodsir Smith. **Nigel Tranter** for the quotes on pages 69, 99 and 122; **Nigel Nisbet** for the Goebbels quote.

Every effort has been made to obtain permission from other copyright holders. The author apologises for any omission.

Michael T.R.B. Turnbull, 1991

Not long ago, I was talking to an Englishman who had settled in Edinburgh many years previously. "It's a wonderful city," he said. "Really most welcoming. They're very happy to say 'Hello' once you've been living next door for ten years..."

You won't find that little tale in the body of this book. But you will find many highly entertaining and often revealing remarks about Scotland's mighty capital. The city once compared to a high-class prostitute - "all fur coat and nae knickers."

I have always loved associating places with words. I remember walking through the streets of Verona with Shakespeare's "Romeo and Juliet" going through my head. Wordsworth came to mind the last time I crossed London's Westminster Bridge. The rolling phrases of the Bible are inescapable when surveying the Holy Land.

Michael Turnbull's diverting volume takes some account of the way poets look at the Athens of the North. But it also allows us to see how all manner of people have been affected by contact with Edinburgh. Playwrights, actors, lawyers, members of the public and even Royalty among them.

It will, obviously, be a book which every tourist should carry when doing the obligatory walk from Castle to Holyrood or admiring the New Town. (How that title baffles incomers who see nothing but very old buildings!)

Their enjoyment of the capital's various historic spots will be greatly enhanced by knowing what others have said about them. When they look at Edinburgh University, for example, will they see what the 19th century surgeon Thomas Tudor Tucker saw - a building "old and irregular and too mean to merit a description?"

But it should also be a part of every Scot's library - especially if he lives in the city, For no one knows less about Edinburgh than the average Edinburger. Most will tell you unblushingly that they've never visited the Castle. Or that they did so once when they took a foreign friend round the city.

Armed with this book, your average Edinburgh family might be tempted to walk around their wonderful, beautiful, infuriating, and lovable city. Matching quotation to place could become a very pleasant and attractive outdoor game.

During the Festival a few years back I interviewed on radio an American who had been coming to Edinburgh every year since 1947. When asked why, he replied: "Because there ain't no place to compare with it anywhere."

He didn't have the benefit of this little volume to help him reach that conclusion. But I'm delighted to put his quote into it!

NEVILLE GARDEN
1991

For Joanna

1
City

IMAGES

Edinburgh has been happily compared with a flag - a thing of history, worn and stained with old deeds and great days, and starred with burning names.
Alanson B. Houghton 1927

Edinborough - The heart of Scotland,
Britaine's other eye.
Ben Jonson (1572-1637)

Auld Reekie! thou'rt a canty hole,   (cheerful)
A bield for mony a caldrife soul   (shelter...cold)
Robert Fergusson 1772

Edina! Scotia's darling seat.
Robert Burns (1759-96)

The City is built between two steep hills, and the Castle on another, so that it may not improperly be compar'd to a spread Eagle.
Joseph Taylor 18th century

Enchanting...it shall make a delightful summer capital when we invade Britain.
Dr. Joseph Goebbels 1938

3

Cities like Edinburgh, far from being mere structures of brick and stone, are living symbols of mankind's fundamental need of faith in co-operative action.

General Dwight Eisenhower 1946

I suppose all the howes and hills and waters of Scotland which creep nearer to Edinburgh in the night look upon her as their Royal Mother.

Sir James M. Barrie 1929

Edinburgh, a blinded giant who has yet to learn
What the motive spirit behind his abilities really is.

Hugh MacDiarmid 1939

The haughty Dun-Edin, the Queen of the North.

James Hogg (1770-1835)
the Ettrick Shepherd

Queen of the unconquered North!

Prof. John Wilson (1785-1854)
alias Christopher North

I view yon Empress of the North
Sit on her hilly throne

Sir Walter Scott (1771-1832)

All my life, Edinburgh has been very near my heart.

Princess Elizabeth 1947

Edinburgh is certainly the most civilised city in Britain. It
has a unique character, charm and grace all its own.
Prince Charles 1990
Grand Steward of Scotland

It is what Paris ought to be
R. L. Stevenson

B E A U T Y

This City is high seated, in a fruitfull soyle,
and wholesome air.
Fynes Moryson (1566-1614)

Nae Heathen Name shall I prefix
Frae Pindus or Parnassus;
Auld Reekie dings them a' to sticks
For rhyme-inspiring Lasses
Robert Burns 1786

it is the dream of a great genius.
B. R. Haydon 1820

I never perceived a better place than Edinburgh. It is
exactly what I fancied it, and certainly is the most
beautiful town in the world.
Benjamin Disraeli 1825

When God Himself takes to panorama-painting, it turns
out strangely beautiful.
Felix Mendelssohn 1829

this delightful and beautiful city
William Cobbett 1832

The view of Edinburgh from the road before you enter
Leith is quite enchanting; it is, as Albert said, 'fairy-like'.
Queen Victoria 1842

this beautiful Auld Reekie
George Eliot 1845

Coming back to Edinburgh is like coming home.
Charles Dickens 1858

our City Beautiful, which had fascinated me in childhood
Patrick Geddes 1880

it is quite lovely - bits of it!
Oscar Wilde 1884

Beautiful city of Edinburgh!
  Where the tourist can drown his sorrow
By viewing your monuments and statues fine
  During the lovely summer-time
William McGonagall 1887

I had never imagined that any city in these islands could be at once so beautiful and fantastic.

J. B. Priestley 1929

well-set Edinburgh

W. H. Auden 1935

Forty-eight years ago I accompanied my husband when you conferred upon him the Freedom of this beautiful city, and I can never forget that occasion. It was my first visit to Edinburgh, the city of my dreams.

Mrs. Louise Carnegie 1935

wife of Andrew Carnegie

I think Edinburgh is the most beautiful city in Europe.

John Betjeman 1957

a city renowned in history and for romance and beauty unsurpassed by any other throughout the whole earth.

Princess Elizabeth 1947

ROMANCE

Mine own romantic town!

Sir Walter Scott

the most magnificent as well as the most romantic of cities.

Maria Edgeworth 1823

ANDREW JOHNSTON'S VIEW OF EDINBURGH.
From the original by de Witt.

I was not yet too old to feel as if I were approaching a great magical city.
Hugh Miller (1802-56)

the city of romance, Edinburgh. Over its cobbled 'causeyed' streets the feet of the wild clansmen have hurried; up its shaded closes their slogans have rung. Round its grim rock wars have raged, and alike in its palaces and towers, and under its humblest roofs, poets have dreamed and lovers have sung. From its barracks men have marched to make the word Freedom great and holy by the shedding of their blood. Through all its grim conflicts there has ever been the urge of the same great liberty. So Edinburgh down history has been the centre and the symbol of things that cannot die.
Sir Harry Lauder 1927

CITADEL

The Castle has been compared with the Acropolis, Arthur's Seat with Mons Hymettus and Leith and Leith Walk with the Piraeus.
Sir John Carr 1807

the city itself, seated proudly amid its hills, raised its picturesque and close-piled masses through the thin haze.

Hugh Miller 1842

An imitation Acropolis is commenced on the Calton Hill and has the effect of the Parthenon.

Nathaniel Parker Willis 1845

The epithets 'Northern Athens' and 'Modern Athens' have been so frequently applied to Edinburgh.

Robert Chambers (1802-71)

Pompous the boast, and yet the truth it speaks
A 'modern Athens,' - fit for modern Greeks

James Hannay 1860

Edinburgh has the proud title of Modern Athens, and she fully deserves it, not only from her natural features and the beauty of her buildings, but from the high level of her intellectual activity.

Lord Joseph Lister 1898

So long as Edinburgh stands on her hill the Scots will never lack their Jerusalem.

John Buchan 1935

Dunedin-Edinburgh-Dunburgh.
A gey done burgh? Wha kens? I daenna.

Eric Gold

HEIGHT

What a wonderful City Edinburgh is! - What alternation of Height & Depth! - a city looked at in the polish'd back of a Brobdignag Spoon, held lengthways - so enormously stretched - up are the Houses!
S. T. Coleridge 1803

In truth, Edinburgh is quite a new phenomenon in the scale of cities. Everything appears original, great, effective.
Frederick Augustus II 1844

It seems like a city built on precipices: a perilous city.
G. K. Chesterton 1905

Far set in fields and woods, the town I see
Spring gallant from the shallows of her smoke,
Cragged, spired, and turreted
R. L. Stevenson

It seemed to me that Edinburgh, the ancient capital of Scotland, enshrined in the affection of the Scottish race all over the world, rich in memories and tradition, immortal in its collective personality, stands by itself.
Sir Winston Churchill 1942

The Scots think of it as their capital; they're too posses-sive, Edinburgh belongs to the world.
Richard Demarco

10

It is a city with nearly everything you want.
Robert Garioch 1959

F IRE AND L IGHT

Edinburgh is a hot-bed of genius.
Tobias Smollett 1776

It was like a city of Chinese lanterns.
Alexander Smith (1830-67)

A city rises before you painted by fire on night.
Alexander Smith

D ARKNESS

Grey metropolis of the North.
Alfred Lord Tennyson (1809-92)

City of mist and rain and blown grey spaces.
Alfred Noyes (1880-1958)

I was born in this city of grey stone and bitter wind.
Ruthven Todd 1940

STONY-HEARTED

'Stony-hearted' Edinburgh! What art thou to me? The dust of thy streets mingles with my tears and blinds me. City of palaces, or of tombs - a quarry, rather than the habitation of men!
William Hazlitt 1822

Edinburgh has become a mere shell of itself, a mere empty tabernacle, a city without a soul.
R. B. Cunninghame Graham 1934

Edinburgh presents outwardly the face it had a hundred years ago, while within it is worm-eaten with all the ingenuity in tastelessness which modern resources can supply.
Edwin Muir 1935

Yes, Edinburgh is a lovely place, for the man who lives on bread alone.
Dominic Behan 1963

As every schoolboy knows, Edinburgh is redolent with history, which in the case of Scotland consists mainly of people knifing one another or blowing up one another's bedrooms.
Cliff Hanley 1963

This rortie wretched city
Sydney Goodsir Smith 1965

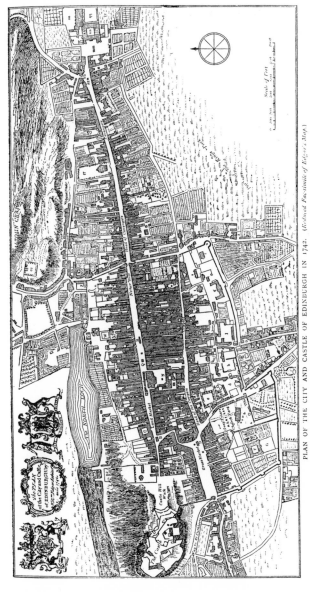

PLAN OF THE CITY AND CASTLE OF EDINBURGH IN 1742. (Reduced Facsimile of Edgar's Map.)

A.—Reservuir.
B.—Weigh House.
C.—James's Court.
D.—Corn Market.
E.—West Port.
F.—Heriot's Hospital.
G.—Bowling Green.
H.—Tolbooth.
I.—Luckenbooth.
K.—Haddows Hole Church and Tolbooth Church.
L.—Old Church.
M.—New Church.
N.—Parliament Close.
O.—Parliament House.
P.—Meat Market.
Q.—The Market Cross.

R.—The Town Guard House.
S.—Fish Market.
T.—Tron Church.
V.—Poultry Market.
W.—Flesh Market.
X.—Upper Market.
Y.—Slaughter-house.
Z.—New Port.

a.—Mary's Chapel.
b.—Magdalen Chapel.
c.—Bowling Green.
d.—Society.
e.—New Gray Friars.
f.—Old Church.
g.—Bristo Port.
h.—Bowling Green.

i.—Argyll's Square.
j.—Trades Hospital.
k.—College.
m.—Potter Row Port.
n.—Bowling Green.
o.—Sreeders' Meeting-house.
p.—Charity Workhouse.
q.—Royal Infirmary.
r.—Chirurgeon's Hall.
s.—Physic Gardens.
t.—High School.
u.—Lady Yester's Church.
v.—Cowgate Port.
w.—The Mint.
x.—Quakers' Burying ground.
y.—Trinity Hospital.
z.—Trinity Church.

aa.—Paul's Work.
bb.—Physic Garden.
cc.—Caltoun Burying place.
dd.—Canongate Flesh Market.
ee.—Canongate Church.
ff.—Churchyard.
gg.—The Girth Cross.
hh.—The Water Gate.
ii.—Physic Gardens.
kk.—Abbey of Holyrood House
ll.—Royal Palace.
mm.—Abbey Close.
nn.—Court.
oo.—Abbey Churchyard.
pp.—Abbey Church.
qq.—Bowling Green.
rr.—Part of St. Anne's Yard.

13

the saturnine Heart of Midlothian, never mine.
Muriel Spark

DESPAIR

I cannot become sadder than I am; a real joy I have not
felt for a long time. Indeed I feel nothing at all; I only
vegetate, waiting patiently for my end.
Frederyck Chopin 1848

City of everywhere, broken necklace in the sun,
you are caves of guilt, you are pinnacles of jubilation.
Norman McCaig

The same Edinburgh I fled from after only three days
because I could not tolerate the litter, the graffiti, the
boarded-up houses. The same Edinburgh where it seems
to be obligatory to board a bus with a can of drink in one
hand and a bag of crisps in the other.
R. Fraser 1986

2
Castle

EDINBURGH CASTLE, FROM THE SOUTH-WEST.
(*Fac-simile of a Dutch Engraving from a Drawing by Gordon of Rothiemay.*)

the Castle of the Maidens
John of Fordun 1093

The castle on a loftie rock is so strongly grounded,
bounded, and founded, that by force of man it can never
be confounded.
John Taylor 1618

the Castle dominates the town
with thunderbolts of war
Arthur Johnston 1642

Edinburgh Castle, elevated in the air, on an impregnable
precipice of rocky earth
Richard Franck 1656

Thy rough, rude fortress gleams afar,
Like some bold veteran grey in arms,
And marked with many a seamy scar:
The pondrous wall and massy bar,
Grim rising o'er the rugged rock
Robert Burns

See yon hoary battlement throned on the rock
James Hogg
the Ettrick Shepherd

Hark, when its sulph'rous vollies fly,
How groans the earth! how roars the sky!
Robert Alves 1789

Such dusky grandeur clothed the height
Where the huge castle holds its state
Sir Walter Scott

I soon found that the rock contained all manner of
strange crypts, crannies and recesses, where owls
nestled and the weasel brought forth her young.
George Borrow (1803-81)

Westward on its sheer blue rock towers up the Castle
of Edinburgh.
Thomas Carlyle (1795-1881)

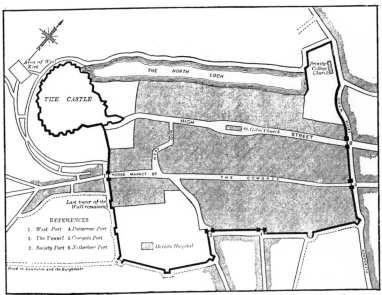

PLAN OF EDINBURGH, SHOWING THE FLODDEN WALL. *(Based on Gordon of Rothiemay's Map, 1647.)*

17

the Castle loomed out dark in the cloud
Hugh Miller (1802-56)

The grandeur of Edinburgh Castle depends eminently on the great, unbroken, yet beautifully varied parabolic curve in which it descends from the Round Tower on the Castle Hill to the terminating piece of independent precipice on the north.
John Ruskin (1819-1900)

I should like to stay there long enough to let the fine landscape of the Castle Rock and Arthur's Seat and Salisbury Crag grow on me.
Gerard Manley Hopkins 1871

Within the last forty years the Castle Hill was a very narrow ridge. The present esplanade was not made, there was no enclosure on either side. There was nothing to obstruct the view between the hill and Princes Street. Not a shrub. It was all open.
Lord Cockburn 1854

the Castle Rock of Edinburgh is, as far as I know, simply the noblest in Scotland conveniently unapproachable by any creatures but sea-gulls or peewits.
John Ruskin 1857

Black-heaved the Castle Rock
Margot R. Adamson

Above all towered the ancient strength of the Castle, battlemented from verge to verge, light as a cloud, insurgent as a wave, massive as its own foundations, etched bold and black against the spreading splendours of the west.

S. R. Crockett (1860-1914)

The Castle looked more than ever a Hallucination, with the morning sun behind it. Or again it had the appearance of a large canvas scenic device such as surrounds Earls Court.

Wilfred Owen

The Castle looms, a fell, a fabulous ferlie.
Dragonish, darksome, dourlie grapplan the Rock
Wi claws o stane.

Alexander Scott

You take photographs of me, I take film of you taking photographs of me!

Crown Prince Akihito of Japan 1961
(with his cine camera to
14 press photographers in the Castle)

The notices are all 'No' this and 'No' that and 'Don't do this' and 'Don't do that' - hardly a warm welcome for the visitor.

Councillor Bill Macfarlane 1983

THE DOGS CEMETERY

Pat VC

Among the dogs buried there is 'Pat VC' (d. 1887) who followed the 72nd Highlanders in peace and war and saved his master, a colour-sergeant, during the Afghan War. When he was attacked by an Afghan, Pat 'bit him on the calf of the leg', for which he was awarded the Dickin Medal.

Bob

'Bob' of the Scots Fusilier Guards took part in the Crimean War - he 'chased the cannonballs and often burned his nose on a hot one'. He was awarded a special silver medal but was run over by a butcher's cart outside Buckingham Palace. Later he was stuffed and put in a glass case.

The Drouthy Elephant

The 78th Highlanders brought a young elephant back from Ceylon in 1839. He was trained to march at the head of the regimental band. One evening his keeper, Private James McIntosh, a Skyeman, went to the canteen for a dram and left the elephant outside. The elephant poked his trunk through the open window and 'drank all the beer and uisgebaugh he was offered'.

TOWERS

All hail thy palaces and towers
Robert Burns

With ancient towers and spiry summits crowned
Thomas Campbell (1777-1844)

Grateful we bow thy gloomy towers before
Victor Hugo (1802-85)

Aft frae the Fifan coast I've seen
Thee tow'ring on thy summit green
Robert Fergusson

21

Edinburgh Castle, toune and toure,
God grant thou sink for sinne!
And that even for the black dinoir
Earl Douglas got therein

old ballad

on the murder of the young sixth Earl of Douglas at the infamous
Black Dinner in Edinburgh Castle, November 1440

3
Old Town

OLD HOUSES IN THE COWGATE, NEAR THE SOUTH BRIDGE, 1850. (*From a Drawing by William Channing.*)

ANIMALS

the Old Town resembles a huge lizard, the Castle its head, church-spires spikes upon its scaly back, creeping up from its lair beneath the Crags.
Alexander Smith (1830-67)

this old black city, which was for all the world like a rabbit-warren, not only by the number of its indwellers, but the complication of its passages and holes.
R. L. Stevenson

a whole serpent-brood of evils, a gorgon's head held up in the sight of the new townsmen, turning their hearts to stone.
Patrick Geddes 1880

old Edinburgh Town, a sloping high-street and many steep side lanes, covers like some wrought tissue of stone and mortar, like some strong rhinoceros skin of stone and mortar....Rhinoceros Edinburgh lies in the mud.
Thomas Carlyle (1795-1881)

The Old Town is a flat fish - the Castle is the head, the Royal Mile the spine; the closes are bones. Holyroodhouse is the tail.
Anon

D A R K N E S S

the Old Town reared its dark brow
Susan Ferrier (1782-1854)

so magnificently picturesque, so old, so gloomy, so individual.
Hans Christian Andersen 1847

I R R E G U L A R I T Y

the rugged, veteran aspect of the Old Town
John Galt (1779-1854)

The old town, with its irregular houses, stage above stage, seen as we saw it, in the obscurity of a rainy day, hardly resembles the work of men, it is more like a piling up of rocks.
Dorothy Wordsworth 1803

ridge on ridge, grey as a rocky coast washed and worn by the foam of centuries
Alexander Smith

jagged, picturesque, piled up
Alexander Smith

Edinburgh was, at the beginning of George III's reign, a picturesque, odorous, inconvenient, old-fashioned town.
Robert Chambers

The spectacle of the old town, seen from the new, is inspiring and splendid, and places Edinburgh, from the artistic point of view, on a level with Constantinople and Stockholm.
John Ruskin 1853

Who could ever hope to tell all its story, or the story of a single wynd in it ?
Sir J. M. Barrie

TENEMENTS

elevations are seven or eight stories high, mounted aloft in the ambient air.
Richard Franck 1656

the bottom of my bed was loose boards, one laid over another, with sharp edges, and a thin bed upon it.
Thomas Kirk 1677

Their old houses are cased with boards, and have oval windows without casements or glass which they open or shut. Their new houses are made of stone, with good windows modestly framed and glazed, and so lofty, that five or six stories is an ordinary height; and one row of

26

buildings there is near the Parliament-Close with no less than fourteen.

Rev. Thomas Mercer 1702

we are settled in convenient lodgings, up four pairs of stairs, in the High Street, the fourth storey being, in this city, reckoned more genteel than the first. The air is in all probability the better; but it requires good lungs to breathe it at this distance above the surface of the earth.

Tobias Smollett 1766

they are generally six or seven stories high in front; but, by reason of the declivity of the hill, much higher backward; one in particular, called Babel, has about twelve or thirteen stories. Every house has a common staircase, and every story is the habitation of a separate family.

Thomas Pennant 1769

The style of building here is much like the French: the houses, however, in general are higher, as some rise to twelve, and in one particular to thirteen stories in height. But to the front of the street nine or ten stories is the common run; it is the back part of the edifice which, by being built on the slope of an hill, sinks to that amazing depth, so as to form the above number.

Captain Edward Topham 1775

I have seen huge Quarries of Lime or Free-Stone, in which the Shafts or Strata have stood perpendicularly instead of horizontally, with the same high Thin Slices, & corresponding Interstices!
S. T. Coleridge 1803

In 1698 a statute of the Scottish Parliament prohibited any house to be built higher than five stories from the ground.
Robert Forsyth 1805

Tier upon tier I see the mansions rise,
Whose azure summits mingle with the skies
Sir Alexander Boswell (1775-1822)

there shot up against the dark sky tall gaunt straggling houses with time-stained fronts, and windows that seemed to have shared the lot of eyes in mortals and to have grown dim and sunken with age. Six, seven, eight storeys high, were the houses; storey piled above storey, as children build with cards.
Charles Dickens (1812-70)

In one room, twelve feet long by ten broad, we once saw twelve women asleep. There was not even straw for them to lie on; but they lay on the boards, such as they were - for they were riddled with rat-holes - with their heads to the creviced wall, and their feet across the chamber.
Dr. George Bell 1849

Within one small apartment, not more than fifteen feet in length by nine in breadth, we found no fewer than eleven persons, all of them grown-up men and women. Four of the inmates, young girls, were in bed, of which there were three. Others sat crouching round a miserable fire, in a state of half-nudity, and with a shawl or petticoat thrown carelessly over the shoulders. The male portion of the company, big hulking fellows, stood with their backs to the fire, or leaned on the edges of the beds. The furniture consisted of a deal table, a few chairs, and a press. The beds were covered with dirty rags of a brown colour, and the effluvia was sickening.

John Heiton 1860

OLD TIMBER-FRONTED HOUSE, LAWNMARKET.

One night I went along the Cowgate after every one was abed but the policeman, and stopped by hazard before a tall land. The moon touched upon its chimneys and shone blankly on the upper windows; there was no light anywhere in the great bulk of building; but as I stood there it seemed to me that I could hear quite a body of quiet sounds from the interior; doubtless there were many clocks ticking, and people snoring on their backs. And thus, as I fancied, the dense life within made itself audible in my ears, family after family contributing its quota to the general hum, and the whole pile beating in tune to its timepieces, like a great disordered heart.

R. L. Stevenson

Those sunless courts, entered by needles' eyes of apertures, congested with hellish, heaven-scaling barracks, reeking with refuse and evil odours, inhabited promiscuously by poverty and prostitution.

Israel Zangwill 1895

Great buildings rush up like rockets

G. K. Chesterton 1905

Cliff-dwellers have poked out from their
High cave-mouths brilliant rags on drying-lines

Norman McCaig 1960

HIGH STREET

the fairest and goodliest streete that ever mine eyes beheld.
John Taylor 1618

the great street, which I do take to be an English mile long, and is the best paved street with boulder stone which are very great ones that I have seen: the channels are very conveniently contrived on both sides of the streets, so as there is none in the middle; but it is the broadest, largest, and fairest pavement, and that entire, to go, ride, or drive upon.
Sir William Brereton 1636

one of the fairest streets I ever saw.
James Howell 1639

it's large and long, and very spacious, whose ports are splendid.
Richard Franck 1656

doubtless the stateliest Street in the World, being broad enough for five Coaches to drive up a-breast.
J Macky 1723

he (Dr. Johnson) acknowledged that the breadth of the street, and the loftiness of the buildings on each side, made a noble appearance.
James Boswell 1773

on each side of this street are Lanes, or Wynds as they are called here, that run down to the bottom. This made an English gentleman merrily compare it to a double wooden Comb, the great Street the wood in the middle, and the Teeth of each side the lanes.

J. Macky 1723

The High Street is also the best pav'd I ever saw. One would think the stones inlaid; they are not half a foot square; and notwithstanding the Coaches and Carts, there is not the least crack in it.

J. Macky 1723

It may be mentioned that, at no very remote time, there were several houses in the Old Town which had the credit of being haunted. It is said that there is one at this day in the Lawnmarket (a flat), which has been shut up from time immemorial. The story goes that one night, as preparations were making for a supper party, something occurred which obliged the family, as well as all the assembled guests, to retire with precipitation, and lock up the house. From that night it has never once been opened, nor was any of the furniture withdrawn: the very goose which was undergoing the process of being roasted at the time of the occurrence, is still in the fire! No one knows to whom the house belongs; no one ever inquires after it; no one living ever saw the inside of it; it is a condemned house!

Robert Chambers

Who could walk through these wonderful buildings
without being conscious that they enshrine the enduring
spirit of a strong stalwart people who have always been
true to themselves?
Princess Elizabeth 1947

Here's where to make a winter fire of stories
And burn dead heroes to keep your shinbones warm
Norman McCaig 1955

SMELL

stink of haddocks and of scaittis
William Dunbar (1460-1520)

I do wonder that so brave a prince as King James should
be borne in so stinking a toun as Edinburgh in lousy
Scotland.
Sir Anthony Weldon 1617

the caution of a man that walks through Edinburgh
streets in a morning, who is indeed as careful as he can
to watch diligently, and spy out the filth in his way; not
that he is curious to observe the colour and complexion
of the ordure, or take its dimensions, much less to be
paddling in, or tasting it; but only with a design to come
out as cleanly as he may.
Jonathan Swift 1696

33

every street shows the nastiness of the Inhabitants, the excrements lye in heaps...In a Morning the Scent was so offensive, that we were forc't to hold our Noses as we past the streets, and take care where we trod for fear of disobliging our shoes, and to walk in the middle at night, for fear of an accident on our heads.
Joseph Taylor 1705

the People were not as willing to live sweet and clean as other nations, but delighted in Stench and Nastiness.
Daniel Defoe 1724

We rode to Edinburgh; one of the dirtiest cities I have ever seen not excepting Cologne in Germany.
John Wesley 1751

a Guide was assigned to me, who went before me to prevent my Disgrace, crying out all the Way, with a loud Voice, Hud your Haunde. The opening up of a Sash, or otherwise opening a Window, made me tremble, while behind and before me, at some little Distance, fell the terrible Shower.
Edward Burt 1754

I smell you in the dark.
Dr. Samuel Johnson 1773

stinking older than the Union
Robert Southey 1819

There was something about the Old Tolbooth which would have enabled a blindfolded person, led into it, to say that it was a jail. It was not merely odorous from the ordinary causes of imperfect drainage, but it had poverty's own smell - the odour of human misery.
Robert Chambers

On stair, wi' tub or pat in hand,
The barefoot housemaids lo'e to stand,
That antrin fouk may ken how snell
Auld Reekie will at mornin' smell:

Then, wi' an inundation big as
The burn that 'neath the Nor' Loch brig is,
They kindly shower Edina's roses,
To quicken and regale our noses.
Robert Fergusson

This accursed, stinking, reeky mass of stones and lime and dung.
Thomas Carlyle 1821

Most of the denizens wheeze, sniffle, and exude a sort of snozzling whnoff whnoff, apparently through a hydrophile sponge.
Ezra Pound

Old Tolbooth

THE TOLBOOTH. (After the Painting by A. Nasmyth.)

In the heart of a great city, it is not accommodated with ventilators, with water-pipe, with privy. The filth collected in the jail is thrown into a hole within the house, at the foot of a stair.

Hugo Arnot 1778

The iron chest measured about nine feet square, and was closed by a strong iron door with heavy bolts and locks. This was the Heart of Midlothian, the condemned cell of the Tolbooth.

James Nasmyth 1817

The floor immediately above the hall was occupied by one room for felons, having a bar along part of the floor, to which condemned criminals were chained, and a square box of plate-iron in the centre, called *the cage*.
Robert Chambers

little dark cells; heavy manacles the only security; airless, waterless, drainless; a living grave.
Lord Cockburn 1840

Antique in form, gloomy and haggard in aspect, its black stanchioned windows opening through its dingy walls like the apertures of a hearse.
Robert Chambers

LAW COURTS

Before 1808, the den called The Inner House then held the whole fifteen judges. It was a low square room, not, I think, above from thirty to forty feet wide. The Barons being next to the sky, had access to the flat leaden roof. The Inner House was so cased in venerable dirt that it was impossible to say whether it had ever been painted.
Lord Cockburn 1840

An immense Hall, dimly lighted from the top of the walls, and perhaps with candles burning in it here and there; all in strange *chiaroscuro*.
Thomas Carlyle

St. Giles

God never had a church, but there, men say,
The divell a chapell hath rais'd by some wyles.
I doubted of this saw, till on a day
I westward spied great Edenbrough's Saint Gyles
William Drummond of Hawthornden

since the Reformation it is turned into four convenient
Churches, by partitions, called the High Kirk, the Old
Kirk, the Tolbooth Kirk, and Haddo's Hole.
J. Macky 1723

THE LANTERN AND TOWER OF ST. GILES'S CHURCH.

the tower above all which rises out of the centre of the
pile, and is capped with a very rich and splendid canopy
in the shape of a Crown Imperial. This beautiful tower
and canopy form a fine point in almost every view of the
city of Edinburgh.
John Gibson Lockhart (1794-1854)

38

What a strange story its old grey crown, as it towers high above the city, tells out day by day to all who have ears to hear.

Rev. Sir James Lees

Edinburgh is a city of churches, as though it were a place of pilgrimage.

R. L. Stevenson

BELLS

Fra sound of St Giles's bell
Never think I to flee

William Dunbar

I observed few bells rung in any of their churches in Edenborough, and, as I was informed, there are but few bells in any steeple, save in the Abbey Church steeple, which is the king's palace.

Sir William Brereton 1636

the excellent Chimes in every steeple, which play a Quarter of an hour together.

Joseph Taylor 1705

Wanwordy, crazy, dinsome thing.

Robert Fergusson

the clock struck nine, and the Evening Roll was heard from the castle-heights. I heard the sound of the drum and the fife.

Rev. Thomas Dibdin 1838

On Tuesday fore-noon November 16th 1824, when all danger seemed to be past, the steeple of the Tron Church was discovered to be on fire. Some burning embers had been carried to the balustrade, and had been fanned into a flame by the wind, which, though it had been calm all night, was now blowing a gale. The steeple was of wood cased in lead, and blazed furiously. The firemen had to fly for their lives, for the molten lead poured down the sides of the structure, and rendered it impossible to approach it with safety. The heat was so great that a large bell weighing two tons, which had been hung in 1673, was fused. The steeple burned for three-quarters of an hour, and then fell with a crash.

W. M. Gilbert 1901

that surprising clamour of church bells that suddenly breaks out on the Sabbath morning, from Trinity and the sea-skirts to Morningside on the borders of the hills.

R. L. Stevenson

The midnight bell vibrating in the Tron.

Margot R. Adamson

In my precipitous city beaten bells
Winnow the keen sea wind.

R. L. Stevenson

THE KRAMES

In my boyhood little stands, each enclosed in a tiny room of its own, and during the day all open to the little footpath that ran between the two rows of them and all glittering with attractions, contained everything fascinating to childhood, but chiefly toys.

Lord Cockburn

LUCKENBOOTHS

As I went by the Luckenbooths
I saw a lady fair
She had long ear-rings in her ears
And jewels in her hair

old song

this would undoubtedly be one of the noblest streets in Europe, if an ugly mass of mean buildings, called the Luckenbooths, had not thrust itself, by what accident I know not, into the middle of the way.

Tobias Smollett

41

MERCAT CROSS

Who are these so dim and wan,
 Haggard, gaunt, and woe-begone!
Who in suits of silvery mail
Wander in the moonlight pale,
Through Dun Edin's narrow street,
  Sad and slow,
And with mournful voice repeat,
  Singing low -
'Dim the night, but dark the morrow -
Long shall last the coming sorrow, -
  Woe to Scotland, woe!'

Charles Mackay
the defeat of Flodden proclaimed from the Cross

Here I stand at what is called the Cross of Edinburgh, and can in a few minutes, take fifty men of genius and learning by the hand.

Mr. Amyat, King's Chemist,
recorded by William Smellie (1740-95)

I was built up in Gothic times,
And have stood several hundred reigns;
Sacred my mem'ry and my name,
For kings and queens I did proclaim.
I peace and war did oft declare,
And roused my country ev'rywhere

James Wilson
alias 'Claudero'

GREAT FIRE OF 1824

Directly over the sea of fire below, the low-browed clouds above seemed as if charged with a sea of blood, that lightened and darkened by fits as the flames rose and fell; and far and wide, tower and spire, and tall house-top, glared out against a back-ground of darkness, as if they had been brought to a red heat by some great subterranean, earth-born fire, that was fast rising to wrap the entire city in destruction.

Hugh Miller 1824

THE OLD TRON CHURCH.

The only remaining danger was from two walls, standing alone, which it was thought a breeze might make smother everything near them. Both were brought down on the Saturday 20th Nov. 1824, one by ropes, and one by powder. The one that was subdued by ropes was near the east end of the south side of the square. It was part of the tallest house in Edinburgh, and was then probably the tallest self-standing wall in Europe being, from the Cowgate, about 130 feet high. It was pulled down by a party of sailors from a frigate in Leith Roads.

Lord Cockburn 1840

43

MARKETS

they suffer a weekly market to be held, in which stalls are
erected nearly the whole length of the High Street and
make a confusion almost impossible to be conceived.
Captain Edward Topham 1775

It was only fifteen or twenty years before that our only
fish market was in Fish Market Close, a steep, narrow,
stinking ravine. The fish were generally thrown out on
the street at the head of the close.
Lord Cockburn

TRINITY HOSPITAL

Narrow stone stairs, helped out by awkward bits of
wooden ones; oak tables of immovable massiveness;
high-backed carved chairs with faded tapestry on their
seats and elbows; a few strong heavy cabinets; drawers
and leaves and bolts and locks and hinges, once the pride
of their inventors, and now exciting a smile at ancient
carpentry; passages on miscalculated levels; long narrow
halls and little inaccessible odd-shaped rooms.
Lord Cockburn

44

GREYFRIARS

A gravedigger, and a friend of his, a gardener from the country, accompanied me into one after another of the cells and little courtyards in which it gratified the wealthy of old days to enclose their bones from neighbourhood. In one, under a sort of shrine, we found a forlorn human effigy, very realistically executed down to the detail of his ribbed stockings, and holding in his hand a ticket with the date of his demise. He looked most pitiful and ridiculous, shut up by himself in his aristocratic precinct, like a bad old boy or an inferior forgotten deity under a new dispensation; the burdocks grew familiarly about his feet, the rain dripped all round him; and the world maintained the most entire indifference as to who he was or whither he had gone.

R. L. Stevenson

Several hundred prisoners taken at Bothwell Bridge were confined here in the open air, under circumstances of privation now scarce credible. They were guarded by day by eight, and through the night by twenty four men; and the soldiers were told that if any prisoner escaped, they should answer it life for life by cast of dice. If any prisoner rose from the ground by night, he was shot at.

Robert Chambers
describing the 17th century Covenanters Prison
in Greyfriars Churchyard

An impressive place. Huge, auld, red, gloomy church; a countless multitude o' grass-graves a' touchin' ane anither.

Prof. John Wilson

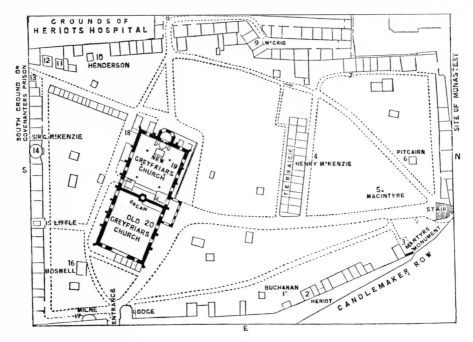

GROUND-PLAN OF GREYFRIARS CHURCHYARD.

References to the Tombs.

1. George Buchanan.
2. George Heriot.
3. Martyrs' Monument.
4. Henry Mackenzie (Man of Feeling).
5. Macintyre (Gaelic poet).
6. Pitcairne (Dr.)
7. Old sculptured monument.
8. Entrance to Heriot's Hospital.
9. M'Crie (biographer of Knox).
10. Alexander Henderson.
11. Adam (of Blairadam).

12. Robertson (historian).
13. South ground (Covenanters' prison),
    Black the chemist, Tytler, etc.
14. Mackenzie (Lord Advocate).
15. Little-Gilmour of Craigmillar.
16. Boswell of Auchenleck.
17. Milne (Master Mason).
18. Allan Ramsay, Maclaurin, Dr. Hugh
    Blair.
19. Lauder and Ruddiman (inside of church).
20. Memorial window to George Buchanan.

Greyfriars is continually overrun by cats. I have seen, one winter afternoon, as many as thirteen of them seated on the grass beside old Milne, the Master Builder, all sleek and fat and complacently blinking, as if they had fed upon strange meats.
R. L. Stevenson

O death where is thy sting
O grave where is thy victory
Tomb inscription
in Greyfriars churchyard

COWGATE

the people of the Cowgate seldom visit the upper streets.
Alexander Smith

The Cowgate will not come to you: you must go to the Cowgate.
Alexander Smith

the filthy, ill-smelling atmosphere of the Cowgate
David M. Moir, 'Delta' (1798-1851)

The Cowgate of Edinburgh resembles much the West Port, but is more decidedly Irish in its character.
James Bruce, Earl of Elgin 1850

47

Admired once by a French ambassador at the court of one of the Jameses, and yet with certain traces of departed splendour, the Cowgate has fallen into the sere and yellow leaf of furniture-brokers, second-hand jewellers and vendors of deleterious alcohol.

Alexander Smith

EDINBURGH UNIVERSITY

The Building is old and irregular, and too mean to merit a description.

Thomas Tucker 1768

The college is a mean building.

Thomas Pennant 1769

What is called the college is nothing else than a mass of ruined buildings of very ancient construction.

Italian visitor 1788

In November 1789 we got a half holiday to see the foundation stone of the new college laid, which was done with great civic and masonic pomp. Forty years did not see the edifice completed.

Lord Cockburn

I can only make sense of this Establishment desert of male tumbleweed by examining my own experience.

Muriel Gray 1988

I liked the ticking of the clock in the Sellar and Goodhart Library, the drop of ash in the grate and the moment when I surfaced into the moonlight world of the Old Quad.

Maida Stainer 1920's

HIGH SCHOOL

High School! - called so, I scarcely know why; neither lofty in thyself nor by position, being situated in a flat bottom; oblong structure of tawny stone, with many windows fenced with iron netting - with thy long hall below, and thy five chambers above, for the reception of the five classes into which the eight hundred urchins, who styled thee instructress, were divided.

George Borrow (1803-81)

That class-room gaunt - those dusky benches hard,
Breech-polished well, with names all over scarred.

anon 19th century

West Bow

The tinkler billies o' the Bow
Are now less eident clinkin
Robert Fergusson

A perfect Z in figure, composed of tall antique houses,
with numerous dovecot-like gables projecting over the
footway, full of old inscriptions and sculpturings, pre-
senting at every few steps some darksome lateral pro-
fundity, into which the imagination wanders without
hindrance or exhaustion.
Robert Chambers

An account of a sword-fight at the West Bow fought in 1596 between
James Johnston of Westerhall and Broad Hugh Somervill of the Writes:

Writes finding himself strucken and wounded, seeing
Westerhall, drawes, and within a short time puttes
Westerhall to the defensive part; for being the taller
man, and one of the strongest of his time, with the
advantage of the hill, he presses him sore. Westerhall
reteires by little, traversing the breadth of the Bow, to

50

gain the advantage of the ascent, to supply the defect of nature, being of low stature, which Writes observeing, keepes closse to him, and beares him in front, that he might not quyte what good-fortune and nature had given him. Thus they continued neer a quarter of ane hour, clearing the causeway, so that in all the strait Bow there was not one to be seen without their shop doores, neither durst any man attempt to red them, every stroak of their swords threatening present death both to themselves and others that should come neer them. Having now come from the head of the Bow neer to the foot thereof, Westerhall being in a pair of black buites,

ASSEMBLY ROOMS, WEST BOW.
(From a Measured Drawing by T. Hamilton, published in 1830).

which for ordinary he wore closse drawen up, he was quyte tyred. Therefore he stepes back within a shop doore, and stood upon his defence. The very last stroak that Writes gave went neer to have brocken his broad sword in peaces, having hitt the lintell of the door, the mark whereof remained there a long tyme. Thereftir, the toune being by this tyme all in ane uproar, the halbertiers

51

coming to seaze upon them, they wer separated and
privatly conveyed to ther chambers. Their wounds but
slight, except for that which Writes had upon his head
proved very dangerous; for ther was many bones taken
out of it; however, at lenth, he was perfectly cured, and
the parties themselves, eftir Hugh Lord Somerville's
death, reconcealled, and all injuries forgotten.

from the **Memorie of the Somervills**

CANONGATE

In Birtley Buildings Midcommon Close, Canongate, a
modern tenement, erected especially for dwellings for
the poor there are 35 rooms, 33 families, 24 children
under five, 101 adults.

Dr Alexander Wood 1868

Down the Canongate
down the Cowgate
go vermilion dreams

Norman McCaig

HOLYROOD

There came under her windows five or six hundred citizens who gave her a concert of the vilest fiddles and rebecs, which are as bad as they can be in that country, and accompanied them with singing psalms, but so wretchedly out of tune and concord that nothing can be worse.
French servant of Mary Queen of Scots 1561

a stately and princely seate
John Taylor 1618

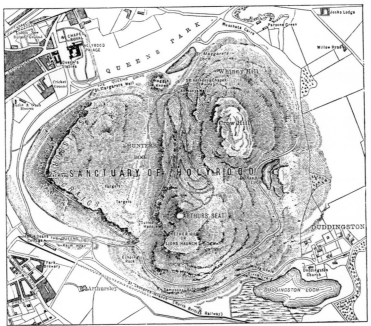

PLAN OF ARTHUR'S SEAT (THE SANCTUARY OF HOLYROOD).

The stately rooms are dirty as stables: the colours of the tapestry are quite faded; several of the pictures are cut and defaced. The roof of the royal chapel is fallen in; and the bones of James the fifth, and the once beautiful Lord Darnley, are scattered about like those of sheep.

Rev. John Wesley 1780

Never, never, I thought, could this once lovely chapel have looked more beautiful than it did at this moment; instead of the pealing notes of the organ, sackbut, harp, lute, and dulcimer, and all the lovely instruments that once resounded through its many arches, it was now pervaded by a still more solemn silence; instead of lighted torches and the innumerable wax tapers that once blazed upon its altars, it was now lighted alone by the stars of heaven.

Countess of Caithness (1830-95)

Palace and ruin, bless thee evermore!

Victor Hugo (1802-85)

The Palace of Holyrood has been left aside in the growth of Edinburgh; and stands grey and silent in a workmen's quarter and among breweries and gas works. It is a house of many memories.

R. L. Stevenson

I saw Holyrood on Sunday afternoon being alone on Salisbury Crags, a floating mirage in gold mist.

Wilfred Owen (1893-1918)

4
New Town

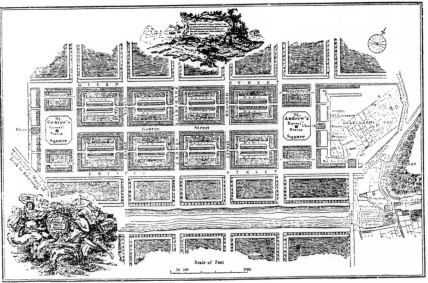

CRAIG'S PLAN OF THE NEW STREETS AND SQUARES INTENDED FOR THE CITY OF EDINBURGH.

heavenly Hanoverianism
Robert Burns

The prospect from the New Town is as beautiful as almost any country can afford. There is a supply of excellent water from the general reservoir; and, in the neighbourhood, there is an inexhaustible fund of free and whinstone quarries, the first for building houses, the last for paving streets.
Hugo Arnot 1778

the buildings are of the finest white stone.
Henry Skrine 1793

the bright, smooth forehead of the New
John Galt (1779-1839)

the New Town stretched its golden lines, white, all around.
Susan Ferrier (1782-1854)

The whole houses are of uniform height, three stories above the street independent of the roof, all executed of the finest hewn stone.
Robert Forsyth 1805

ST. STEPHEN'S CHURCH.

It was then an open field of as green turf as Scotland could boast of, with a few respectable trees on the flat, and thickly wooded on the bank along the Water of Leith...how can I forget the glory of that scene on the still nights on which I have stood in Queen Street, or the opening of the north-west corner of Charlotte Square, and listened to the ceaseless rural corn-craiks nestling happily in the dewy grass.

Lord Cockburn 1822

the New Town arose, growing from day to day, until
Edinburgh became one of the most handsome and
picturesque cities in Europe.

James Nasmyth (1808-90)

I am aware of no streets which, in simplicity and manli-
ness of style, or general breadth and brightness of effect,
equal those of the New Town of Edinburgh.

John Ruskin 1853

It is as much a matter of course to decry the New Town
as to exalt the Old; and the most celebrated authorities
have picked out this quarter as the very emblem of what
is condemnable in architecture....
It cannot be denied that the original design was faulty and
short-sighted, and did not fully profit from the capabili-
ties of the situation. The architect was essentially a town
bird and he laid out the modern city with a view to street
scenery, and to street scenery alone.

R. L. Stevenson

at the time of the building of the new town imperfect
notions prevailed as to the internal and external drainage
of houses. The domestic use of baths was apparently
unknown and the conveniences were few in number and
awkwardly placed. The drainage escaped in all directions,
infiltrating the neighbouring soil, undermining it everywhere and aiding the operations of those persevering
tunnellers, the rats.

Dr. Henry Littlejohn 1863

the pale blue misty twilight of Edinburgh streets

S. R. Crockett

THE MOUND

Another communication between the centre of the city and the New Town of Edinburgh has of late years been opened, by means of a mound of earth laid from the Lawn-market across the North Loch. This mound was made passable for carriages in three years. It is above 800 feet in length. On the north it is 58 feet in height, and on the south 92.

Robert Forsyth 1805

PRINCES STREET

The first thoroughfare, now a magnificent terrace, was called St. Giles Street, after the ancient patron of the city; but on the plan being shown to George III for his approval, he exclaimed, "Hey, hey! - what, what! - St. Giles Street! - never do, never do!" And so, to escape from a vulgar London association of ideas, it was named Princes Street, after the future Duke of York.

James Grant 1883

The street is furnished, like all the principal streets of Edinburgh, with a broad smooth pavement of hewn stone on each side for foot passengers, and the centre with a strong causeway of basaltic blue stone, called whinstone. It is obtained in abundance from the neighbouring rocks of Arthur Seat.

Robert Forsyth 1805

Princes Street in a clear sun-set with the Castle and the Pentland Hills in radiant glory was a sight perfectly original.
B. R. Haydon 1820

There is no street in Europe more spectacular than Princes Street, where all the hotels stand in a row. Princes Street was absolutely operatic.
Henry James 1878

Princes Street, that noblest of earthly promenades
S. R. Crockett

In twos and threes, they have not far to roam,
Crowds that thread eastward, gay of eyes;
Those that seek no further than their quiet home,
Wives, walking westward, slow and wise.
Wilfred Owen

Among the tea-rooms in Princes Street there are places more strange than a dream.....They excite or depress the senses to the limit of endurance and pour non-alcoholic drinks on the resulting commotion. The pubs are, in comparison, civil and humane institutions.
Edwin Muir

Princes Street is a sort of schizophrenia in stone.
Eric Linklater 1960

SCOTT MONUMENT

I am sorry to report the Scott Monument a failure. It is like the spire of a Gothic church taken off and stuck in the ground.

Charles Dickens

The wise people of Edinburgh built...a small vulgar Gothic steeple on the ground, and called it the Scott Monument.

John Ruskin

THE ASSEMBLY ROOMS

we actually drilled our two companies almost every night during the four winter months of 1804 and 1805, by torchlight, in the ground flat of the George Street Assembly Rooms, which was then all one earthen-floored apartment

Lord Cockburn 1840

BELLEVUE

No part of the scenery of Edinburgh was more beautiful than Bellevue, the villa of General Scott. It seemed to consist of nearly all the land between York Place and Canonmills - a space now almost covered by streets and houses. The whole place waved with wood, and was diversified by undulations of surface, and adorned by seats and bowers and summer houses. Nothing certainly, within a town, could be more delightful than the sea of the Bellevue foliage gilded by the evening sun, or the tumult of blackbirds and thrushes sending their notes into all the adjoining houses in the blue of a summer morning.

Lord Cockburn 1840

5
Suburbs

LEITH ROADS, 1824. (*After a Drawing by J. Galletly.*)

Suburbs

Day by day, one new villa, one new object of offence, is added to another; all around Newington and Morningside, the dismallest structures keep springing up like mushrooms; the pleasant hills are loaded with them, each impudently squatted in its garden, each roofed and carrying chimneys like a house.

R. L. Stevenson

Duddingston

Overhung by the green slopes and grey rocks of Arthur's Seat, and shut out by its mountainous mass from every view of the crowded city at its further base in Duddingston, a spectator feels himself sequestered from the busy scenes which he knows to be in his immediate vicinity, as he hears their distant hum on the passing breezes by the Willow Brae on the east, or the gorge of the Windy Goule on the south; and he looks southward and west over a glorious panorama of beautiful villas, towering castles, rich coppice, hill and valley, magnificent in semitint, in light and shadow, till the Pentlands, or the lonely Lammermuir ranges, close the distance.

anon 1851

DUDDINGSTON LOCH.

Duddingston Loch lies under the abrupt southern side of
Arthur's Seat; in summer, a shield of blue, with swans
sailing from the reeds; in winter, a field of ringing ice.
R. L. Stevenson

With caws and chirrupings, the woods
In this thin sun rejoice,
The Psalm seems but the little kirk
That sings with its own voice
R. L. Stevenson

PRESTONFIELD

Joys of Prestonfield, adieu !
Late found, soon lost, but still we'll view
Th' engaging scene - oft to these eyes
Shall the pleasing vision rise.

Cheerful meals, balmy rest,
Beds that never bugs molest,
Neatness and sweetness all around
These at Prestonfield we found
Dr Benjamin Franklin 1759

CRAIGMILLAR

Upon Craigmillar's regal walls,
The blackbird's mellow vesper lay;
Proclaims meet dirge of closing day
James Fraser 1817

NIDDRIE

Niddrie House, the garden! unseen and unseeing, it was
a world of its own. That unwalled flat space, of only four
or five acres, contained absolutely everything that a
garden could supply for "man's delightful use"; peaches
and oaks, gravel walks, and a wilderness "grotesque and
wild," a burn and a bowling-green, shade and sun, covert
and lawn, vegetables and glorious holly hedges - everything delightful either to the young or the old. Eden was
not more varied. And Eden is well worthy of its reputation
if it was the scene of greater happiness.
Lord Cockburn 1840

FAIRMILEHEAD

The air comes briskly and sweetly off the hills, pure from the elevation and rustically scented by the upland plants; and even at the toll, you may hear the curlew calling on its mate. At certain seasons, when the gulls desert their surfy forelands, the birds of sea and mountain hunt and scream together in the same field at Fairmilehead.

R. L. Stevenson

WATER OF LEITH

the banks of the river were bounded by tangled brakes of bramble and hawthorn. The water was pure, and abounded with different species of minnow, and in some parts with fine trout.

Cumberland Hill 1887

The Water of Leith
where all the ladies clean their teeth

William McGonagall

St Bernard's Well

This water so healthful near Edinburgh doth rise
Which not only Bath but Moffat outvies.
Most diseases of nature it quickly doth cure.

It cleans the intestines and appetite gives
While morbific matter it quite away drives
'Claudero' 1760

St Bernard's House

This interesting old house was surrounded by large
green fields, a fine orchard of apple and pear trees, and
leading from this was another avenue of old stately elms.
Margaret Ferrier 1820

Ann Street

It is an almost unique experience to walk down Ann
Street - originally, as it were, a village street - on a
summer day and see - like a Greek temple in a cottage
garden - the form and symmetry and elegance of the
houses set off by the little informal gardens, the green
shrubs and trees, the roses nodding on their stems.
Professor A. J. Youngson

MORNINGSIDE

But, now that I come to think of it, Edinburgh was not all education and cable-cars. It was a place where top-hats were very much in vogue, like feather-boas; where church-bells rang authoritatively; where to speak "Scotch" was unfortunate, to say the least of it; where the residents of the southern suburbs of Marchmont and Morningside used to pull down their front-window blinds on the 11th of August, for a fortnight, and retire to the back rooms - to give the impression that they had departed North for the grouse-shooting.

Nigel Tranter

SWANSTON

The road goes down through another valley, and then finally begins to scale the main slope of the Pentlands. A bouquet of old trees stands round a white farmhouse; and from a neighbouring dell, you can see smoke rising and leaves ruffling in the breeze.

R. L. Stevenson

COLINTON

It was a place in that time like no other; the garden cut
into provinces by a great hedge of beech, and overlooked
by the church and the terrace of the churchyard, where
the tombstones were thick, and after nightfall 'spunkies'
might be seen to dance, at least by children; flower-pots
lying warm in sunshine; laurels and the great yew making
elsewhere a pleasing horror of shade; the smell of water
rising from all round, and an added tang of papermills; the
sound of water everywhere, and the sound of mills - the
wheel and the dam singing their alternate strain; the birds
of every bush and from every corner of the overhanging
woods pealing out their notes until the air throbbed with
them; and in the midst of this, the manse.

R. L. Stevenson
describing Colinton Manse

Here is the mill with the humming of thunder,
Here is the weir with the wonder of foam
R. L. Stevenson

CRAIGCROOK

In 1815 Francis Jeffrey set up his rustic household gods
at Craigcrook. No unofficial house in Scotland has had a
greater influence on literary or political opinion.
Lord Cockburn 1840

morally the Paradise of Edinburgh.
Lord Cockburn 1854

So old, yet so comfortable; so picturesque and so sensible; so beautifully small within the garden, but with such rich soft over turf outside. What a wood-grown hill.
Lord Cockburn 1854

PORTOBELLO

At Portobello the soft glow
Of azure tide expands,
For there the waves of ocean flow
On its smooth shelving sands
James Costelloe 1878

us twa, bob-bobbin amang the fresh, cool, murmurin, and faemy wee waves, temperate as the air within the mermaid's palace
Prof. John Wilson
alias 'Christopher North'

Portobello presents a charming seaboard, extending for many hundreds of yards, gently sloping to the briny wave, and covered with silvery sand. Can it be believed, then, that this lovely beach has its silver sand percolated by all the common foetid sewers of this fashionable bathing town? Monstrous? But it is a fact.
'A Northern Bear' 1854

It was wonderful to see the vast number of dead Sea-mice and Cuttle-fishes strewed along the shore, especially after rough weather.
George Stephenson M.D. 1918

my song, my shanty
east-coast town, last resort
of the terminally out-of-season
Andrew Greig 1982

LEITH

This town of Leith is built all of stone, but it seemeth to
be but a poor place, though seated upon ainty haven: the
country 'twixt this and Edenborough, and all hereabout
this city, is corn.
Sir William Brereton 1636

The first year, the oysters were sold at 4s per barrel. The
price has risen gradually, and now mounts to 6s. In AD
1778, 8,400 barrels were exported, which at 6s per
barrel, amounts to £2,520. Thus it appears, if the oyster-
banks on the Forth are not dragged more sparingly, this
commodity will be speedily exhausted.
Hugo Arnot 1779

Leith, with its thicket of masts, and its tall round Tower.
Hugh Miller

Go, fetch to me a pint o' wine,
And fill it in a silver tassie;
That I may drink before I go,
A service to my bonnie lassie.

The boat rocks at the pier o' Leith;
Fu' loud the wind blaws frae the Ferry
Robert Burns

72

Leith camps on the seaside with her forest of masts;
Leith roads are full of ships at anchor
R. L. Stevenson

LEITH PIER, FROM THE WEST, 1775.

when a cargo of claret came to Leith, the common way
of proclaiming its arrival was by sending a hogshead of it
through the town on a cart, with a horn; and anybody
who wanted a sample, or a drink under pretence of a
sample, had only to go to the cart with a jug, which,
without much anxiety about its size, was filled for
sixpence.
Lord Cockburn 1840

SIGNAL TOWER, LEITH PIER, 1775. (After Clerk of Eldin.)

73

GRANTON

The abhominations of Granton Pier, with its tram-
roads, brickwork and quarry
Lord Cockburn 1797

Granton Pier is the first rival to Leith on the south side
of the Firth of Forth and will probably produce a
considerable change in the trade of carrying goods and
passengers to Edinburgh.
Lord Cockburn 1838

On the oily skin of the water
Are coils and whorls, all oily
Norman McCaig 1963

CRAMOND

Nether Cramond is a thriving village, containing 87
families and 343 individuals, chiefly iron workmen, sailors and day labourers. The harbour has belonging to it
seven sloops of from 22 to 80 tons burthen, measuring
in all 288 tons and navigated by 23 men. These are chiefly
employed in the importation of lime for manure, coals
and iron for the mills and in exporting steel and wrought
iron.
John Wood 1794

From Wardie to Cramond was all open fields, fringed
on the seashore with whins
Lord Cockburn

FORTH

Slide soft, fair Forth, and make a crystal plain
William Drummond of Hawthornden

Wha'll buy my caller herrin'
New drawn frae the Forth
Lady Caroline Nairne (1766-1845)

that glorious Forth, all silent, serene, sublime
Prof. John Wilson
alias 'Christopher North'

6
Gardens

THE PALACE OF HOLYROOD HOUSE (33). THE SOUTH AND NORTH GARDENS (33). THE ABBEY KIRK (2)
AND THE KIRKYARD (2). (*After Gordon of Rothiemay's Plan.*)

PHYSIC GARDEN

On the north of the city in a bottom, is the Physic Garden with 2,700 sorts of plants, as the Keeper of it told me.
Rev. Thomas Morer 1702

DEAN CEMETERY

How the savages were smashing the wood today, as if for mere pleasure! I thought that venerable trees and undying evergreens were exactly what a burial-ground would long for. Here they are in perfection - plenty hollies and yews, apparently a century old; and how did I see these treated? As a drove of hogs would treat a bed of hyacinths.
Lord Cockburn 1845
On the construction of the Dean Cemetery

PRINCES STREET GARDENS

The vital improvement of enclosing, draining and ornamenting the valley to the west of the Mound as part of the North Loch was completed in 1820. The place had just been sufficiently drained to prevent its ever again being a loch. But it was a nearly impassable fetid marsh, a stinking swamp, open on all sides, the receptacle of many sewers, and seemingly of all the worried cats, drowned dogs, and blackguardism of the city.
Lord Cockburn 1840

What are now gardens, planted and maintained by a local assessment, and consequently most justly enclosed, was a fetid and festering marsh, the receptacle for skinned horses, hanged dogs, frogs, and worried cats.

Lord Cockburn 1854

And our Trees ! where are they? There is no element in the composition of town scenery so valuable; and I could name at least eight, but more probably a dozen, of places within the city, that I remember being graced by very respectable groups of them, well placed and well growing. Had not beams been the only forms in which house-builders like wood, the whole of them might have been preserved. Not a twig of them lives.

Lord Cockburn 1854

I went down to the station of the North British Railway yesterday, and took my last look of the few remaining fragments of Trinity Hospital, and of the trees which still mark "where once a garden smiled." There is one good ash, a large willow, an admirable elm and two hawthorns. The elm stands on the north-west angle of the old Physic Gardens and might be quite easily saved. The hawthorns were in their grave-clothes of beautiful flourish. I suppose they are all down now.

Lord Cockburn 1845

The Princes Street Gardens, so exquisitely beautiful in themselves, instead of offering a quiet and refreshing refuge to weary souls, are marred by the shrieking, snorting engines of a railroad that spreads its hideous tracks and vile-smelling smoke through their very centre.

Maria H. Landsdale

Trees. More trees. Oh more trees!
Big John Duncan 1991

THE MEADOWS

There has never in my time been any single place in or
near Edinburgh, which has so distinctly been the resort
at once of our philosophy and our fashion. Under these
trees walked, and talked, and meditated, all our literary
and scientific, and many of our legal worthies.
Lord Cockburn

7
Hills

Edinburgh, like Prague, is situated on a hill
Alexander Alane 1550

Install'd on hills, her head near starry bowers,
Shines Edinburgh, proud of protecting powers
William Drummond of Hawthornden

thy summit green
Robert Fergusson

Calton Hill, Arthur's Seat and the adjoining eminences, afford retreats where the gravest philosopher may indulge his contemplations; the melancholy mourner, sequestered from the prying eyes of busy curiosity, pour forth his sighs in silence to the passing winds; or the enraptured poet catch inspiration.
Vincenzo Lunardi 1785

Ye mountain-walks, Edina's green domain
Thomas Campbell (1777-1844)

When I was a boy nearly the whole vicinity of Edinburgh was open. Beyond the Causeway it was almost Highland. Corstorphine Hill, Braid Hill, Craiglockart Hill, the Pentland Hills, the seaside from Leith to Queensferry.
Lord Cockburn 1845

Stately Edinburgh throned on crags
William Wordsworth (1770-1850)

the hills covered here and there with tufts of blooming
whins, as yellow as beaten gold.

David M. Moir

Nothing can abolish the hills, unless it be a cataclysm of
nature which shall subvert Edinburgh Castle itself and lay
all her florid structures in the dust.

R. L. Stevenson

ARTHUR'S SEAT

a hill with two heads called of Arthur, The Britain
Arthur's Chair

James Brome 1669

Let me to Arthur's Seat pursue,
Where bonnie pastures meet the view,
And mony a wild-lorn scene accrues

Robert Fergusson

Arthur's Seat shall be my bed,
The sheets shall ne'er be press'd by me;
St. Anton's well shall be my drink,
Sin' my true-love's forsaken me

old song

Have I not experienced the full force of the wild grandeur
of nature when gazing at thee, O Arthur Seat, thou
venerable mountain! whether in the severity of winter

thy brow has been covered with snow or wrapped in mist; or in the gentle mildness of summer the evening sun has shone upon thy verdant sides diversified with rugged moss-clad rocks.

James Boswell (1740-95)

I climbed last night to the Crags just below Arthur's Seat, itself a rude triangle-shaped bare Cliff, & then looked down on the whole City & Firth, the Sun the setting behind the magnificent rock, crested by the Castle - the Firth was full of Ships, & I counted 54 heads of mountains, of which at least 44 were cones or pyramids - the smoke rising up from ten thousand houses, each smoke from one family - it was an affecting sight to me! I stood gazing at the setting Sun, so tranquil to a passing Look, & so restless & vibrating to one who looks steadfast; & then all at once turning my eyes down upon the City, it & all its smokes & figures became at once dipped in the brightest blue-purple - such a sight that I almost grieved when my eyes recovered their natural Tone!

S. T. Coleridge 1803

the Mountain, like a lion couchant, reposing in the sky

Prof. John Wilson

alias 'Christopher North'

a high hill, very rocky at the top, and below covered with smooth turf, on which sheep were feeding.

Dorothy Wordsworth (1771-1855)

Arthur's Seat was perfect witchcraft

Washington Irving 1817

If I were to choose a spot from which the rising or setting sun could be seen to the greatest possible advantage, it would be that wild path winding around the foot of the high belt of semicircular rocks, called Salisbury Crags, and marking the verge of the steep descent which slopes down into the glen on the south-eastern side of Edinburgh.

Sir Walter Scott 1818

When standing at the 'Giant's Ribs,' on the south side of Arthur's Seat, I felt as if one of the grandest pages of the Earth's history lay open before me.

James Nasmyth

These are the columnar masses of rock which form the face of Salisbury Crags. There is a legend that one day one of these pillars will fall and crush the greatest man that ever passes under them.

Dr. Oliver Wendell Holmes 1834
describing Samson's Ribs

When I first scrambled to that cliff, which must have been about 1788, the path along its base was certainly not six feet wide, and in some places there was no regular path at all. By 1816 the cliff had been so quarried away that what used to be the footpath was, in many places, at least 100 feet wide; and if this work had been allowed to go on for a few years more, the whole face of the rock would have disappeared. This would have implied the obliteration of some of the strata which all Edinburgh ought to have revered as Hutton's local evidence of the Theory of the Earth, and one of the most peculiar features of our scenery.

Lord Cockburn 1840

old Arthur's Seat, towering, surly and dark, like some
gruff genius.
                        Charles Dickens

we can see the huge back of Arthur's Seat faint and grey
amid the haze.
                        Hugh Miller

A huge uneven pennon of fire flared on the summit of
Arthur's Seat, lighting up its own swart trail of smoke
with an umbry red, and converting into a vast halo, of
more than a thousand yards diameter, the mist-wreaths
that brooded there.
                        Hugh Miller 1842

THE HERMITAGE OF BRAID

Would you relish a rural retreat,
Or the pleasure the groves can inspire,
The city's allurements forget,
To this spot of enchantment retire
                        Robert Fergusson

Braid burn Towlies
Morningside Swine
Tipperlinn's the bonnie place
Where a' the leddies dine
                        old song

86

CALTON HILL

The Calton, blackened by its moving thousands, resembled a huge ant-hill just stirred.
Hugh Miller 1842

The upper part of it was frequently occupied as a place for beating carpets with flails, which sent clouds of insanitary dust over the neighbouring ground. On the north slope linen was washed and the ground slopped around water-cocks which should never have been allowed to disfigure the scene. The washings were hung up on poles stretched on shabby, badly set-up poles, disfiguring the view.
Lord Kingsburgh (1836-1919)

The scene suggests reflections on fame and on man's injustice to the dead. You see Dugald Stewart rather more handsomely commemorated than Burns. Immediately below, in the Canongate churchyard, lies Robert Fergusson, Burns's master in his art, who died insane while yet a stripling; and if Dugald Stewart has been somewhat too boisterously acclaimed, the Edinburgh poet, on the other hand, is most unrightously forgotten.
R. L. Stevenson

The Calton Hill is the glory of Edinburgh. It has excellent walks; it presents us with the finest prospects both of the city, its vicinity and the distant objects; and it is adorned by beautiful buildings, dedicated to science and to the memory of distinguished men.
Lord Cockburn 1854

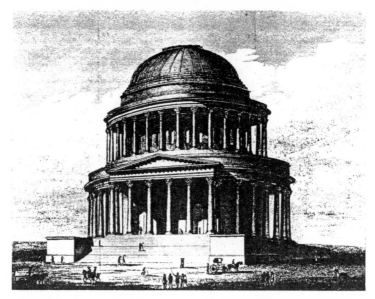

PERSPECTIVE VIEW of the NATIONAL MONUMENT

the National Monument is often referred to as 'Scotland's pride and poverty'. The pillars are of gigantic proportions, formed of beautiful Craigleith stone; each block weighed from ten to fifteen tons, and each column as it stands, with the base and frieze, cost upward of £1,000. As a ruin it gives a classic aspect to the whole city. According to the original idea, part of the edifice was to be used as a Scottish Valhalla.

James Grant 1883

windflaucht, weet Parnassus
Eric Gold

BLACKFORD HILL

Blackford! on whose uncultured breast,
Among the broom, and thorn, and whin,
A truant-boy, I sought the nest
Sir Walter Scott

CORSTORPHINE HILL

(Craigcrook Castle) is on the eastern slope of Corstorphine Hill, about three miles to the north-west of Edinburgh. When Francis Jeffrey first became the tenant, the house was only an old keep, respectable from age, but inconvenient for a family; and the ground was merely a bad kitchen garden, of about an acre; all in paltry disorder. He immediately set about reforming. Some ill-placed walls were removed; while others, left for shelter, were in due time loaded with gorgeous ivy.
Lord Cockburn 1852

The north-west end of Corstorphine Hill, with its trees and rocks, lay in the heart of this pure radiance, and there a wooden crane, used in the quarry below, was so placed as to assume the figure of a cross; there it was, unmistakable, lifted up against a crystalline sky. All three gazed at it silently. As they gazed, he gave utterance in a tremulous, gentle, and rapid voice, to what all were feeling, in the word 'Calvary !'
John Brown M.D.
on the novelist W. M. Thackeray (1811-63)

89

THE PENTLANDS

The Pentlands are smooth and glittering, with here and there the black ribbon of a dry-stone dyke, and here and there, if there be wind, a cloud of blowing snow upon a shoulder.

R. L. Stevenson

I shall never take that walk by the Fisher's Tryst and Glencorse. I shall never see Auld Reekie. Do you know where the road crosses the burn under Glencorse Church? Go there and say a prayer for me. See that it is a sunny day; I would like it to be Sunday; ...stand on the right bank just where the road goes down into the water, and shut your eyes; and if I don't appear to you...

R. L. Stevenson

And if people sit up all night in lone places on the hills, with Bibles and tremulous psalms, they will be apt to hear some of the most fiendish noises in the world: the wind will beat on doors and dance upon roofs for them, and make the hills howl around their cottage with a clamour like the judgement day.

R. L. Stevenson

On three sides of Edinburgh, the country slopes downward from the city, here to the sea, there to the fat farms of Haddington, there to the mineral fields of Linlithgow. On the south alone, it keeps rising until it not only out-tops the Castle but looks down on Arthur's Seat. The character of the neighbourhood is pretty strongly marked by a scarcity of hedges; by many stone walls of varying height; by a fair amount of timber; by here

90

and there a little river, Esk or Leith or Almond, busily journeying in the bottom of its glen; and from almost every point, by a peep of the sea or the hills. There is no lack of variety, and yet most of the elements are common to all parts; and the southern district is alone distinguished by considerable summits and a wide view.

R. L. Stevenson

I think I never saw anything more beautiful than the ridge of Carnethy against a clear frosty sky, with its peaks and varied slopes. The hills glowed like purple amethyst; the sky glowed topaz and vermilion colours. I never saw a finer series than the Pentlands, considering it is neither rocky nor highly elevated.

Sir Walter Scott

take my compliments to your master, and tell him that I cannot sup with him tonight.

Captain James Wallace

shout to Tam Dalyell's cavalry who were pursuing him after the battle of Rullion Green 1666

Here and nar to this piece, lyes the Reverend Mr John Crookshanks and Mr Andrew McCormock ministers of the Gospel and about 50 other true Covenanted Presbyterians who were killed in this place in their own inocent self defence and defence of the Covenanted work of Reformation by Thomas Dalyell of Bins upon the 28th November 1666. Rev 12.11

Inscription on the Martyrs Tomb at Rullion Green c.1730

Wee pursued in the dark, killed all the foot and but for the night and steep hills had wholly destroyed them. Some prisoners are fitt for examples. I do not know how many but I conjecture not above 140, for there was sound payment.

Our losse I cannot tell, but it is greater than their skins were worth, their number was about 15 or 1600 and would without doubt encreased if God had not confounded their imaginacions and rebellious dispositions. Upon Monday the rebells swore the covenant at Lenrick and all to die in defence of it, most of these who led their troops were cashiered preachers.

Now I trust your grace is at ease. I am.

Yr Grces
most obedient and humble servt

W. Drummond

General William Drummond describing the aftermath of the battle of Rullion Green in a letter to John Leslie, 1st Duke of Rothes

8
Weather

The weather is raw and boisterous in winter, shifty and ungenial in summer, and downright meteorological purgatory in the spring.
R. L. Stevenson

MORNING

Perceivet the morning blae, wan, and haar,
With cloudy gum and rack o'erwhelmed the air
Gavin Douglas (1475-1522)

Now morn, wi' bonnie purple-smiles
Kisses the air-cock o' St Giles
Robert Fergusson

When I look out in the morning, it is as if I had waked up in Utopia.
George Eliot 1852

I love cool pale morning,
In the empty bye-streets
R. L. Stevenson

DUSK

the pallid bleakness of the street
In the chill dusks that harry northern June
Margot R. Adamson

NIGHT

I love night in the city,
The lighted streets and the swinging gait of harlots
R. L. Stevenson

The grimy spell of the nocturnal town
R. L. Stevenson

The heady
Darkness swirls with tenements
Norman McCaig

The night tinkles like ice in glasses
Norman McCaig

STARS

For many hours they walked about in the streets, gazing
up at the glittering windows, some of which looked as if
a constellation of stars had come down for a night to
adorn them.
Catherine Sinclair 1815

It was the year of the famous comet, and of the still more
famous vintage, the year 1811; the weather was fine, and
often hot; not one drop of rain fell all the time I was in
Edinburgh. The nights were clear and bright; we often
contemplated the stranger comet from Princes Street;

and not only the comet, but the ordinary array of the shining hosts of heaven.
Thomas Jefferson Hogg (1792-1826)

WIND

The wind made wave the red weed on the dike
Gavin Douglas

Wide where with force so Aeolus shouts shrill
In this congealit season sharp and chill,
The caller air, penetrative and pure,
Dazing the blood in every creature
Gavin Douglas

the winds, instead of rushing down with impetuosity, whirl about in eddies, and become still more dreadful. On these occasions it is almost impossible to stir out of doors, as the dust and stones gathered up in these vortices not only prevent your seeing, but frequently cut your legs by the velocity with which they are driven. The Scotch have a particular appellation for this, 'The Stour'.
Edward Topham (1751-1829)

The bitter east
Alfred Lord Tennyson (1809-92)
from The Daisy which was written in Edinburgh

Calton Hill where every breeze is health
Lady Caroline Nairne

Let us try whether a breeze on the Calton Hill will not dispel these cobwebs from your brain.
Susan Ferrier

Lo! stately Streets, lo! Squares that court the breeze!
James Thomson (1700-48)

Winter is come again, and Edinburgh is beginning once more to look like herself, like her name and nature, with rain, mist, sleet, haur, hail, snow I hope, wind, storm - would that we could but add a little thunder and lightning - The Queen of the North.
Prof. John Wilson
alias 'Christopher North'

Edinburgh pays cruelly for her high seat in one of the vilest climates under heaven. She is liable to be beaten upon by all the winds that blow, to be drenched with rain, to be buried in cold sea fogs out of the east, and powdered with the snow as it comes flying southward from the Highland hills.
R. L. Stevenson

belching winter wind
R. L. Stevenson

97

nirly, nippin', Eas'lan' breeze
R. L. Stevenson

windy parallelograms
R. L. Stevenson

You go to dinner, the east wind is blowing chillily from hostess to host. You go to church, a bitter east wind is blowing in the sermon.
Alexander Smith (1830-67)

there is something almost physically disgusting in the bleak ugliness of easterly weather.
R. L. Stevenson

The Scots dialect is singularly rich in terms of reproach against the winter wind. Snell, blae, nirly and scowthering are four of these significant vocables; they are all words that carry a shiver with them.
R. L. Stevenson

blown grey spaces
Alfred Noyes

the wind whistles through the town as if it were an open meadow; and if you lie awake all night, you hear it shrieking and raving overhead with a noise of shipwrecks and falling houses.
R. L. Stevenson

this city of grey stone and bitter wind.
Ruthven Todd 1940

the "east-windy, west-endy" city with its feet in the sea
and its head in the hills
Nigel Tranter

RAIN

some canker'd biting shower
Robert Fergusson (1750-74)

the missile rain
R. L. Stevenson

City of mist and rain
Alfred Noyes

a street sloe-black in the rain
Karl Miller

HAAR/FOG

the morning blae, wan and haar
Gavin Douglas

haar o' seas
R. L. Stevenson

City of mist and rain.
Alfred Noyes

The heicht o the biggins is happit in rauchens o haar.
Alexander Scott

And outside like chrysanthemums
The fog unfolds its bitter scent
Norman McCaig

SNOW

Edinburgh, with her satellite hills and all the sloping
country, is sheeted in white. The Pentlands are smooth
and glittering, with here and there the black ribbon of a
dry-stone dyke, and here and there, if there be a wind,
a cloud of blowing snow upon a shoulder. The Firth
seems a leaden creek.
R. L. Stevenson

9
Life and Death

COVENANTER'S FLAG.

RELIGION

To Jupiter, the best and greatest of the gods, the 5th Cohort of Gauls, under the command of Lucius Minthonius Tertullus the prefect, gladly, willingly and duly fulfilled the vow.

Second century inscription on an altar
from the **Roman Fort at Cramond**

From May 27th 1661, that the most noble Marquis of Argyle was beheaded, to the 17th of February 1688 that Mr. James Renwick suffered; were one way or other Murdered and Destroyed for the same Cause, about Eighteen thousand: of whom were executed at Edinburgh, about an hundred of Noblemen, Gentlemen, Ministers and others; noble Martyrs for Jesus Christ. The most of them lie here.

Inscription on **The Martyrs Monument**
in Greyfriars churchyard

The cloven foot for which thou art worshipped I despise; yet I remember thee with affection. I remember that, in spite of vain philosophy, of dark doubts, of toilsome learning, God has stamped his image of benignity so strong upon thy heart, that not all the labours of thy head could efface it.

Mrs. Cockburn 1764
in a letter to David Hume

The healthy creative force will break through
Even in Edinburgh - and good, human things grow,
Protecting and justifying faith
In regeneration to a free and noble life
When labour shall be a thing
Of honour, valour, and heroism
And "civilisation" no longer like Edinburgh
On a Sabbath morning,
Stagnant and foul with the rigid peace
Of an all-tolerating frigid soul!
                    Hugh MacDiarmid

Music

When he visited Edinburgh, he appeared immensely
pleased at being escorted from the Caledonian Station
by a pipe band, provided by his impresario, and those
who witnessed the scene long remembered the beaming
face of the tall, broad-shouldered tenor, as he strode
through the station to the accompaniment of the roll of
the drums and skirl of the pipes. So delighted was he with
his reception that he at first proposed to appear at his
concert in Highland costume!
                    Description of the visit of
                    Enrico Caruso
                    who sang at the McEwan Hall in 1909

In 1964 the Beatles gave a concert in the city and were
entertained by the Lord Provost:
'Just like America' commented John Lennon about his
enthusiastic reception.
'Have you got one for Ringo?' Paul McCartney asked the
Lord Provost who had shown him his chain of office.
Eric Taylor, assistant manager of the group, added 'The
boys are thrilled to bits with Edinburgh and would like to
have seen more of it'.

SCULPTURE

There were present at the unveiling a vast number of
pensioners drawn up in the street, many minus legs and
arms, while a crowd of retired officers , all wearing the
newly-given war medal, occupied the steps of the Register House, and were cheered by their old comrades to
the echo. Many met on that day who had not seen each
other since the peace that followed Waterloo; and when
the bands struck up such airs as "The garb of old Gaul"
and "The British Grenadiers" many a withered face was
seen to brighten, and many an eye grew moist.

Descrition of the unveiling of
the Duke of Wellington's statue
from **James Grant's** Old and New Edinburgh

THE WELLINGTON STATUE, REGISTER HOUSE.

Mid lightning's flash and thunder's echoing peal,
Behold the Iron Duke, in bronze, by Steell.

An epigram written on the unveiling of the equestrian statue of
the Duke of Wellington at the east end of Princes Street
in 1852 during a thunder-storm

ART

Art is for everyone - paint, like a piece of music, is the most international thing I know.

Richard Demarco

LITERATURE

No Sculptur'd marble here, no pompous lay,
No storied Urn, no animated Bust,
This simple Stone directs pale Scotia's way,
To pour her sorrows o'er her poet's dust.

Robert Burns
lines written at the grave of
Robert Fergusson in the Canongate Kirk

Here it was that the Ursa Major of literature stayed for a few days, in August 1773, while preparing to set out to the Hebrides, and also for some time after his return. Here did he receive the homage of the trembling literati of Edinburgh.

Robert Chambers on **Dr Johnson**

I feel a sense of security here. If I felt that Edinburgh was threatened with too much destruction I would not have decided to end my days in this city.

Sir Compton Mackenzie 1954

ARCHITECTURE

Princes Street is a medley of plastic and glass frontages jostling with each other.

Dr. Elder Dickson 1954

In 1968 one of the finest examples in Scotland of Venetian baroque architecture - the Life Association building at the foot of the Mound in Princes Street - was scheduled for demolition. **Colin McWilliam**, the architectural historian, vowed to lie down under the bulldozers. Even the foreman of the demolition team commented that it was the 'best bit of stone-carving in the street'. After the demolition had been carried out he added: 'Our business is in ruins!'

St Andrew Square was a 'disgraceful mess - you cannot tell whether you are in Edinburgh, Glasgow, Hull, Hell or Halifax'.

John Cameron 1954

DRAMA

Whaur's yer Wullie Shakespeare noo?
Shout from a delighted member of
the audience at the first performance of
John Home's Douglas, a Scottish tragedy

DRINK

Younger's Edinburgh Ale... a potent fluid, which almost glued the lips of the drinker together, and of which few, therefore, could dispatch more than a bottle.
Robert Chambers

The SWEATING CLUB flourished about the middle of the last century....After intoxicating themselves, it was their custom to sally forth at midnight, and attack whomsoever they met upon the streets. Any luckless wight who happened to fall into their hands was chased, jostled, pinched, and pulled about, till he not only perspired, but was ready to drop down and die with exhaustion.
Robert Chambers

POLITICS

Under no circumstances will I ever again be a candidate for Edinburgh
Thomas Babington Macaulay (1800-1859)

Medicine

He comes in, sits down with a little, a very little, bob of a bow, rubs his trousers with both hands open, and signs for the first case. The four dressers on duty, and in aprons, march in if possible in step, carrying a rude wicker basket, in which, covered by a rough red blanket, the patient peers up at the great amphitheatre crammed with faces. A brief description and then the little, neat, round-shouldered, dapper man takes his knife and begins.

Description of Professor James Syme
the 'Napoleon of Surgery'

Suddenly there was a talk of sounds being heard like those of a cotton mill, louder and louder; a moment more, then all was quiet, and then - a crash.

Dr James Young Simpson
discovering the anaesthetic properties of chloroform at his home in Queen Street in 1847

Mankind is responsible for tuberculosis. What an ignorant civilisation has introduced, an educated civilisation can remove.

Sir Robert Philip
the conqueror of tuberculosis

BEGGARS

Your Burgh of beggaris is ane nest,
To schout and swen youris will nocht rest;
All honest folk they do molest,
Sa piteuflie thai cry and rame:
Think ye nocht schame,
That for the poore hes no thing drest,
In hurt and sclander of your Name!
William Dunbar

TOWN COUNCIL

the Council Chambers were in a low-roofed room, very
dark and very dirty, with some small dens off it for clerks.
Within this Pandemonium sat the town-council,
omnipotent, corrupt, impenetrable.
Lord Cockburn

REPUTATION

How does it feel to be the sexiest man alive?
There are very few sexy ones dead
Sean Connery 1991
at a press conference before receiving the Freedom of the city

110

LADIES OF THE NIGHT

There was at that period a well-known house known as the Cock and Trumpet, for the reason that a bantam was represented on the sign as blowing a clarion of war in the shape of a huge French horn. Going straight in and passing through a room of sleeping beauties reposing amidst a chorus of snorts, I came to the bed-room. The mistress was enjoying in bed the repose due to her midnight and morning labours, snoring as deep as a woman of her size and suction could do.

James McLevy
Victorian detective pursuing stolen goods in a
well-known Edinburgh house of ill repute,
now Acheson House

LINTEL ABOVE THE DOOR OF SIR A. ACHESON'S HOUSE.

Groups of sorrily dressed women flaunting about, smelling of bad hair and worse perfumes, sitting on ricketty chairs, or lounging on legless sofas, with a patched carpet covering the room, and the paper peeling off from a severe attack of damp.

J G Bertram 1864
describing an Edinburgh brothel

Nowhere that I have been is one so bathed and steeped and rolled about in floating sexual desire as in certain streets of Glasgow and Edinburgh. This desire fills the main thoroughfare and overflows into all the adjacent pockets and backwaters: the tea-rooms, restaurants and cinema lounges.

Edwin Muir

A letter of protest from a Danube Street resident in 1977 described 'being woken up by drunken louts banging on the front door; once by a beer can flung at that same time while its owner vomited on the doorstep; once by a girl screaming outside the bedroom window, the screams accompanied by a deafening cacophony of barking, running dogs.'

The reply of the madam, **Dora Noyes** 'the oldest girl in the oldest profession' was that her establishment 'was just like a YMCA really, with a few extras....Edinburgh is a very old fashioned city, of course. There's nothing to do after 10 o'clock at night.'

POLITICAL PRISONERS

When our ashes shall be scattered by the winds of heaven, the impartial voice of future times will re-judge your verdict.

Thomas Muir
the political martyr at his trial in 1793
He was transported to Botany Bay.

John Maclean, the Socialist activist, spent a month in Edinburgh's Calton Jail as Convict No. 2652. In Russia **Lenin** wrote that Maclean had 'been sentenced to 18 months imprisonment with hard labour for fighting against the predatory British Bourgeoisie.'

LAWYERS AND JUDGES

The Londoner, when he visits Edinburgh, is astonished to find that it possesses a Valhalla filled with gods - chiefly legal ones - of whose names and deeds he was previously in ignorance.
Alexander Smith

Lift the sneck and draw the bar:
Bluidie Mackinye, come out if ye daur!
Doggerel rhyme shouted by schoolboys
into the Mausoleum of Sir George Mackenzie
in Greyfriars churchyard

I am almost alone in the midst of its swarms, and am disturbed by its filth and debauchery and restraint, without having access to much of the virtue or genius it may contain.
Francis Jeffrey (1773-1850)

This judge had a predilection for pigs. One, in its juvenile years, took a particular fancy for his lordship, and followed him wherever he went, like a dog, reposing in the same bed. When it attained the mature years and size of swinehood, this of course was inconvenient.
However, his lordship, unwilling to part with his friend, continued to let it sleep at least in the same room, and, when he undressed, laid his clothes upon the floor as a bed to it. He said that he liked it, for it kept his clothes warm till the morning.

Robert Chamber's
description of Lord Gardenstone

Firm, wiry and muscular, inured to active exercise of all kinds, a good swimmer, an accomplished skater, and an intense lover of the fresh breezes of heaven. He was the model of a high-bred Scotch gentlemen.

Lord Cockburn
as described by The Edinburgh Review 1857

Strong built and dark, with rough eyebrows, powerful eyes, threatening lips, and a low growling voice. He once said to an eloquent culprit at the bar - "Y're a vera clever chiel, man, but ye wad be nane the waur o' a hanging".

Robert MacQueen, Lord Braxfield (1722-99)
as described by Lord Cockburn.
Braxfield presided over the Deacon Brodie trial
and sent the political reformer, Thomas Muir,
to Botany Bay.

When his lordship found his end approaching very near, he took a public farewell of his brethren. I was informed by an ear and eye witness, who is certain that he could not be mistaken, that, after addressing them in a solemn speech, and shaking their hands all round, in going out of the door of the court-room he turned about, and casting them a last look, cried, in his usual familiar tone: "Fair ye a' weel, ye bitches!"

Robert Chambers'
description of Lord Kames

In former times, it was the practice of the Lord President to have a sand-glass before him on the bench, with which he used to measure out the utmost time that could be allowed to a judge for the delivery of his opinion. Lord President Dundas would never allow a single moment after the expiration of the sand, and he has often been seen to shake the old-fashioned chronometer ominously in the faces of his brethren, when their ideas on the subject began to get vague and windy.

Robert Chambers

We are told that there was no malice, and that the prisoner must have been in liquor. In liquor! Why, he was drunk! And yet he murdered the very man who had been drinking with him! They had been carousing the whole night; and yet he stabbed him; after drinking a whole bottle of rum with him; Good God, my Laards, if he will do this when he's drunk, what will he not do when he's sober?

George Fergusson, Lord Hermand (died 1827)
quoted by Lord Cockburn.
Hermand was a great believer in the
beneficial effects of claret and punch.

115

CAPITAL PUNISHMENT

Dr. Johnson: 'Sir, never talk of your independency, who could let your Queen remain twenty years in captivity, and then be put to death, without even a pretence of justice, without ever attempting to rescue her.'
James Boswell (1740-95)

Oh! soon, to me, may summer-suns
Nae mair light up the morn!
Nae mair, to me, the autumn winds
Wave o'er the yellow corn!
And in the narrow house o' death
Let winter round me rave;
And the next flow'rs, that deck the spring,
Bloom on my peaceful grave!
Robert Burns
Lament of Mary Queen of Scots

'Why weep ye so, ye burgess wives,
Why look ye so on me?
O, I am going to Edinburgh town,
A rich wedding for to see.'

When she gaed up the Tolbooth stairs,
The corks frae her heels did flee;
And lang or e'er she came down again,
She was condemn'd to die
Scott's Border Minstrelsy
The Queen's Marie

Let them bestow on ev'ry Airth a Limb;
Open all my Veins, that I may swim
To Thee my Saviour, in that Crimson Lake;
Then place my pur-boil'd Head upon a Stake;

Scatter my Ashes, throw them in the Air;
Lord since Thou know'st where all these Atoms are
I'm hopeful, once Thou'lt recollect my Dust,
And confident Thou'lt raise me with the Just.

James Graham, Marquis of Montrose (1612-50)
who fought against the Covenanters but was finally captured,
executed at Edinburgh's Mercat Cross and his body disposed of as
he so well predicted.

The wild-flowers wave
Above the lowly bed of others, who,
Although less known to fame, resistance made
In liberty's defence
Anon
the Covenanters' grave in Greyfriars churchyard

At the trial he had appeared in a full dress-suit of black
clothes, the greater part of which was of silk, and his
deportment throughout the affair was composed and
gentlemanlike. He continued during the period which
intervened between his sentence and execution to dress
well, and keep up his spirits. A gentleman of his
acquaintance, calling upon him in the condemned room,
was surprised to find him singing the song from the
Beggars' Opera, 'Tis woman seduces all mankind'. Having
contrived to cut out a draughtboard on the stone floor
of his dungeon, he amused himself by playing with any
one who would join him, and, in default of such, with his

right hand against his left. The diagram remained in the room where it was so strangely out of place till the destruction of the jail. His dress and deportment at the gallows (October 1, 1788) displayed a mind at ease, and gave some countenance to the popular notion that he had made certain mechanical arrangements for saving his life. Brodie was the first man who proved the excellence of an improvement he had formerly made on the apparatus of the gibbet. This was the substitution of what is called the drop, for the ancient practice of the double ladder. He inspected the thing with a professional air, and seemed to view the result of his ingenuity with a smile of satisfaction. When placed on that insecure pedestal, and while the rope was adjusted round his neck by the executioner, his courage did not forsake him. On the contrary, even there he exhibited a sort of levity; he shuffled about, looked gaily around, and finally went out of the world with his hand stuck carelessly into the open front of his vest.

Robert Chambers

But still, by the mind's eye, he may be seen, a man harassed below a mountain of duplicity slinking from a magistrates supper room to a thieves' ken, and pickeering among the closes by the flicker of a dark lamp.

R. L. Stevenson

HANGMAN'S HOUSE AT FOOT OF FISHMARKET CLOSE IN 1824 —
FROM ENGRAVING BY THE RELIEF COMMITTEE.

The last Edinburgh executioner of whom any particular notice has been taken by the public was John High, commonly called Jock Heich, who acceded to the office in the year 1784, and died so lately as 1817. High had been originally induced to undertake this degrading duty, in order to escape the punishment due to a petty offence - that of stealing poultry. I remember him living in his official mansion in a lane adjoining to the Cowgate - a small wretched-looking house, assigned by the magistrates for the residence of this race of officers, and which has only been removed within the last few years.

Robert Chambers

119

The fatal day was announced to the public by the appearance of a huge black gallows-tree towards the eastern end of the Grassmarket. This ill-omened apparition was of great height, with a scaffold surrounding it, and a double ladder placed against it, for the ascent of the unhappy criminal and the executioner.

Sir Walter Scott

EAST END OF THE GRASSMARKET, SHOWING THE WEST BOW,
THE GALLOWS, AND OLD CORN MARKET.
(Fac-simile of an Etching by Jame Skene of Rubislaw.)

Then e'en let him glorify God in the Grassmarket!
John Leslie, 1st Duke of Rothes 1666
to an unrepentant Covenanter

Up the close and doun the stair
But and ben wi' Burke and Hare.
Burke's the butcher, Hare's the thief,
Knox the boy that buys the beef.

A popular rhyme

written after the Burke and Hare case 1829, the two body-snatchers
who supplied the anatomist Dr. Robert Knox with
bodies for dissection.

Great was the throng to see him hung,
For crimes that were so vile;
To Edinburgh upon that day
They tramped for many a mile.
They led him out all clad in black -
Black coat and vest so white -
A mocking smile was on his lips;
He wore a nosegay bright.

A popular rhyme

on the case of William Benison, executed in 1850 for bigamy and the
murder of his wife.

Chantrelle eyed its sombre furnishings with seeming
interest, and unflinchingly took his stand beneath the
rope.

A description of **Eugene Chantrelle** in the Calton Jail
death chamber. He was a teacher of French
executed in 1878 for poisoning his wife

SCHOOLDAYS

Of my boyhood I need say little, save that it was spartan at home and more spartan at the Edinburgh school where a tawse-brandishing schoolmaster of the old type made our young lives miserable. From the age of seven to nine I suffered under this pock-marked, one-eyed rascal.

Sir Arthur Conan-Doyle (1859-1930)

Every morning at precisely 8.35 I left my home in Eyre Crescent down near Canonmills, and reluctantly started the long ascent to learning - up Pitt Street, up Dundas Street, up Hanover Street, across Princes Street, up the Mound steps, up through Lady Stair's Close, along George IV Bridge, Forrest Road and Lauriston Place, to George Heriot's School. If the First Bell, at 8.57, was still ringing as I came in sight of the august 17th century institution, I had thrown away precious moments of freedom by leaving the house too early; if the Second Bell, at 9 o'clock was just stopping, I had cut it a mite fine.

Nigel Tranter

MEMORY

I have exceedingly early and rather extended recollections in connection with this ancient city - this most interesting and beautiful city.

On the occasion of my first visit to it I heard the glass of the windows of the Royal Hotel rattle to the guns of the Castle, as they announced one of the great victories won over Napoleon the Great, in the year 1815.

William E. Gladstone (1809-98)

10
Festival

THE MUSIC HALL, GEORGE STREET

What was seen at the time as Edinburgh's 'first modern Music Festival' was held beside St Giles in the Parliament House in 1815. One memorable feature was what *The Edinburgh Courant* described as 'the gigantic burst of harmony which thundered from the organ, and all the other instruments'. Lord Cockburn commented 'We have become an infinitely more harmonious nation'. The 1855 Festival held in the Music Hall, George Street, was equally well attended - 'every portion of the spacious room, even to the orchestra and passages, being densely crowded.'

The Edinburgh International Festival of Music and Drama was born during the course of a conversation between Rudolf Bing and H. Harvey Wood in a Hanover Square restaurant in London. Back in Edinburgh the Countess of Rosebery and Lord Provost Falconer conspired to coax the Edinburgh International Festival into life. Since that time visitors and residents alike have given their verdict on Edinburgh and its annual influx of 'culture'.

One square mile of Edinburgh has, for three weeks, been the artistic centre of the world.
Rudolf Bing 1948
Artistic Director of the Festival

Edinburgh has always been regarded as a city of culture.
Lord Provost John Falconer 1947

I count it among my most precious recollections. It had a deeply moving character and a unique charm.
Artur Schnabel 1947

I see in all this the culmination of a great literary and cultural revival.

John Grierson 1947

I have no space left to enlarge on the friendliness and hospitality with which the visitor to Edinburgh is greeted. The atmosphere is perfect. One has the sense of a great and ancient city which cares about the arts.

E. M. Forster 1947

These chandeliers are worth coming across the Atlantic to see.

an American woman 1948

bewitched by the Music Hall Festival Club

I feel Edinburgh ought to have an orchestra of its own.

Fritz Busch 1950

Edinburgh, my very old love.

Sir John Barbirolli 1950

The Assembly Hall ? I hate it!

Fay Compton 1953

playing Queen Gertrude to Richard Burton's Hamlet
at the Assembly Hall

What you have seen here in Edinburgh is one of the most magnificent experiences since the war. Here, human relations have been renewed.

Dr Bruno Walter 1953

125

When I come out of the Waverley Station, I feel I am home.

Henry Sherek 1953

I believe that the ordinary man in the street in Edinburgh has no idea of the reputation of the Festival overseas. If he knew how many people look to Edinburgh as a great international gathering place for the great arts and artists then he would be very much prouder than he is.

Robert Ponsonby 1956

Edinburgh Festival audiences applaud everything with equal indiscrimination!

Sir Thomas Beecham 1956
conducting the Royal Philharmonic at the Usher Hall

I deeply regret we have not finished yet.

Sir Thomas Beecham 1956
to an Usher Hall audience that clapped too soon.

It must have been over 30 years ago that I combined the learning of golf and the playing of Shaw in a six-week season at Edinburgh. I bought my first club in Edinburgh, and I believe I still have it.

Wilfrid Lawson 1959
played in Sean O'Casey's
Cock-a-Doodle Dandy at the Lyceum

I travelled up here by train and car and when I got here
I was on the verge of whining with fatigue.
Dame Edith Sitwell 1959
who gave readings at the Lyceum Theatre

A gracious and lovely city.
Pandit Nehru 1961

I have tried many times to grow a Himalayan poppy at
home, with no success!
Sherpa Tensing Norkay 1963
on being presented with the curious present of a Himalayan poppy
grown in Edinburgh

The Edinburgh Festival is a flash in the pan!
Duncan Macrae 1965
appearing as the Porter in Macbeth at the
Assembly Hall

An absolute yearly glory.
Lennox Milne 1965
doyenne of Scottish drama

I love being in Edinburgh.
Jane Asher 1966
appearing as Perdita in The Winter's Tale at the Assembly Hall

a memorable stay among the worst back-stage facilities
in Britain.
Laurence Harvey 1966
describing the Assembly Hall, where he appeared as Leontes

127

I was touring with the Bristol Old Vic during a harsh winter, when one night at the King's, during a full house, the trams went off because of the weather. We plodded home in wellington boots and I think we were stranded here for about three days.

Wendy Hiller 1966
who appeared in A Present for the Past at the Lyceum

I must say I would rather be handed a flower than have an atom bomb thrown at me.

Jennie Lee 1967
Minister for the Arts

The set-up from every point of view is delightful.

David Frost 1968

The dining room closes on the stroke of ten like Stalag VII. You've got to crawl out under the wire.

Dick Lester 1969
on a well-known Princes Street hotel

I always love to come to Edinburgh - this magnificent city.

Lillian Gish 1969
who presented her recollections of a lifetime's work in the cinema at the Cameo picture-house

Can Edinburgh ever become the Rio de Janeiro of the North?

Richard Eyre 1971

Edinburgh has made me one of her citizens and I'm grateful. This is one of the loveliest cities in the world.
Yehudi Menhuin 1971
who played with the Scottish
National Orchestra at the Usher Hall

Edinburgh to me always seems like a Scandinavian Capital. It's very different from England and very refreshing.
Peter Ustinov 1972

It's a forbidding city in many ways. The main thing is that Edinburgh doesn't really change. I much prefer it with wild Valkyrian clouds over the Castle.
Joseph Losey 1972

it is great to be back in Edinburgh again.
Sir Geraint Evans 1973
who played Leporello in Mozart's
Don Giovanni at the King's Theatre

Edinburgh is one of my three favourite cities. It's as beautiful as Florence or Prague.
Joan Bakewell 1974

the Edinburgh Tattoo is a great attraction. Parts of it are very moving.
Edward Heath 1975

I arrived in Edinburgh this morning, but so far I love the place.

Burt Lancaster 1976

I've never seen so many people falling about in the streets at night in my life. It's robust. It's raw. It's got a lot going for it.

Diane Cilento 1976
Australian actress formerly married to Sean Connery

It's a beautiful town. It's not a town, it's a city.

Ronnie Scott 1976

I walked down Princes Street yesterday and there was a very festive air. The gardens are really beautiful.

Princess Grace of Monaco 1976
reading poetry at St Cecilia's Hall to commemorate
the American bi-centenary

Hello Edinburgh ! I'm here at your wonderful Festival and me a scruff fae Glasgow.

Billy Connolly 1976

Some place this! Look at the size of it. You can get a licence to shoot antelopes in the balcony.

Billy Connolly 1976
on the Playhouse Theatre

130

I think it is one of the greatest things which has ever happened in Scotland and, as a man from the Wild West, I just wish that Glasgow had thought of it first.
Jack House 1976

To say that Edinburgh gets a world-class Festival on the cheap is an under-statement.
Peter Diamand 1976

I often feel that the Festival itself desperately needs a Busby Berkeley.
Billy Connolly 1977

I'm always delighted to be here. I'm very much an 18th century chap.
Frank Muir 1977
reading in He and She at St Cecilia's Hall

The great thing about the Festival is meeting people and the non-stop talking.
Joan Bakewell 1977

To see the Castle and Princes Street in the sun and a clear blue sky, it's got to be magic.
Pete Murray 1979

I used to think there was a lot wrong with Edinburgh....by seven in the evening all the chairs were piled on the tables in the Princes Street cafes.
Richard Baker 1979

Last night was fine for me. That hall has a great sound.
Oscar Peterson 1980
on the Usher Hall

The city lacks gaiety when the Festival's not on.
Alfred Marks 1980
who played Falstaff with the Royal Shakespeare Company

It's a marvellous ethos to have a festival in. It has a scholarly feel. Anything that's built on rock generates force.
Michael Bentine 1981

Buns and cheap wine were the order of the day.
Lord Harewood 1981
Festival Director

It would seem to me that the Festival is not wanted.
John Drummond 1983
Festival Director

Every so often you need a jolt to the system.
Frank Dunlop 1983
theatrical producer (and, later, Festival Director)

The living arts are in great danger from the awful glass eye.
Dr Jonathan Miller 1984
on the Television Festival

I've always regarded Edinburgh with enormous
affection. I love this city.
Peter O'Toole 1984
patron of Marmont Productions' A Sleep of Prisoners

Dublin and Edinburgh both have an indefinable perfume
and I love the way you've absorbed the foreigners.
Peter Ustinov 1984

You tell Edinburgh people about its reputation through-
out the world, but they just don't believe it.
Andrew Cruickshank 1984
Chairman of the Fringe

The Festival must be beyond factional dispute.
Frank Dunlop 1985

I feel I'm abroad when I'm here.
Russell Harty 1985

When you come back each time it looks so classy.
Ronnie Corbett 1985

You couldn't have a festival of this enormity and scale in
London because you couldn't control or contain all the
movement.
Sean Connery 1986

133

The Kinetic Sculpture was a waste of money, £11,000, and an eyesore, as was that pile of old tyres in Princes Street Gardens.

Mrs. Rita Carson 1986

The Spring Fling is good for our city, don't knock it. Let's give it our entire support ... including the rubber Parthenon!

Donald Smith 1986
Director of the Netherbow Arts Centre

Do we ever do anything in Edinburgh except create holes in the ground and bicker about them?

Colin Bell 1986

I look on it as one big family party.

Humphrey Lyttleton 1987

I have five hundred ideas.

Frank Dunlop 1991
outgoing Festival Director

11
Farewell

Farewell, my bonny, lovely, witty, pretty Maggy,
And a' the rosy lasses milking on the down:
Adieu the flowery meadows, aft sae dear to Jocky,
The sports and merry glee of Edinborrow town.
Allan Ramsay (1686-1758)

But, Sir, let me tell you, the noblest prospect which a
Scotchman ever sees, is the high road that leads him to
England!
Dr Samuel Johnson

Auld chuckie Reekie's sair distrest,
Down droops her ance wel-burnisht crest,
Nae joy her bonnie buskit nest,
Can yield ava,
Her darling bird that she lo'es best,
Willie's awa!
Robert Burns
An epistle to William Creech, his publisher
with whom relations were not always cordial

I feel as if there would be less sunshine for me from this
day forth.
Sir Walter Scott 1821
at the funeral of the publisher John Ballantyne

Ae fond kiss, and then we sever;
Ae fareweel, alas for ever !
Robert Burns
lines written to Mrs. Nancy Maclehose when they corresponded as
Sylvander and Clarinda

Clarinda, mistress of my soul,
The measur'd time is run!
The wretch beneath the dreary pole
So marks the latest sun.
To what dark cave of frozen night
Shall poor Sylvander hie;
Depriv'd of thee, his life and light,
The sun of all his joy?

Robert Burns

To Clarinda, on the poet's leaving Edinburgh

And often to myself, in whispers weak,
I breathe the name of some dear gentle maid,
Of some loved friend, whom in Edina's shade
I left, when forced these eastern shores to seek.
And for the distant months I sigh in vain,
To bring me to those favourite haunts again.

John Leyden (1775-1811)

Farewell, Edina ! pleasing name, -
Congenial to my heart !

Thomas Campbell

This morning I leave No. 93 Castle Street for the last
time. 'The cabbin was convenient' and habit had made it
agreeable to me. I never reckoned upon a change in this
particular so long as I held an office in the Court of
Session. In all my former changes of residence it was
from good to better - this is retrograding. I leave the
house for sale and I cease to be an Edinburgh citizen in
the sense of being a proprietor - which my father and I
have been for sixty years at least.

Sir Walter Scott 1826

the old time is dead also, never, never to revive. It was a sad time too, but so gay and so hopeful, and we had such sport with all our low spirits and all our distresses, that it looks like a kind of lamplit fairyland behind me.

R. L. Stevenson 1881

An open cab came slowly towards us, westward along Princes Street ... As it passed us, a slender, loose garbed figure stood up in the cab and waved a wide-brimmed hat.

"Goodbye!" he called to us. "Goodbye!"

"It is Louis Stevenson!" said my companion; "they must be going away again."

The cab passed. The grey vista of our Northern Capital, the long line of Princes Street, was at its very best as Louis Stevenson looked back at it ... It was Edinburgh's last sight of Louis Stevenson, and Louis Stevenson's last look back at the city that was his birthplace.

Flora Masson

Yet when the lamp from my expiring eyes
Shall dwindle and recede, the voice of love
Fall insignificant on my closing ears,
What sound shall come but the old cry of the wind
In our inclement city?

R. L. Stevenson

Appendix A
EDINBURGH JOKES

When you go into a house in Glasgow they ask you: "What would you like for tea?"
In Edinburgh they say to you: "You'll have had your tea?"

Homesick - an exile from Edinburgh bursting a paper bag at one o'clock.

A wee Edinburgh bunny decided to go to London to see what it was like, but he soon came home. When he was asked why he'd come home, he answered "Jings there's nae dry-burras doon there"

Two tigers were walking down Princes Street - one says to the other:
"Quiet for a Saturday, isn't it?"

An Edinburgh councillor decided to take an early morning tour of Leith Docks. It was freezing cold and he badly needed to 'spend a penny'. He saw a docker and went up to him: 'Excuse me, my man, " he said. Could you tell me where the urinal is?" The docker looked blank and the replied "Couldnae tell ye, Jim. How many funnels has she got?"

MORNINGSIDE AND COMELY BANK *(Kimly Benk)*

Q. What's SEX in Morningside?
A. The bags they deliver coal in.

Q. Do you have trouble with RATES in Morningside?
A. No, we only have mice.

LEITH - *Rhyming Slang*

Leith Street hag - fag
White Star Liner - joiner
Are you Cable's Wynd? - blind
Port o' Leith - teeth
Tongue-Twister - The Leith Police dismisseth us

FOOTBALL

One Saturday afternoon an American tourist stood in Princes Street for the first time and asked a passer-by: "Where's this Castle of yours?"
"At your back".
"And the Scotch Monument?"
"In front of you".
"And where's Edinburgh's disgrace?"
"O them! They're playing away the day".

Appendix B
SPEAKIE-REEKIE

bag - a noun meaning unlikable woman as in 'she's a twisted, moany-faced old bag'

bag off - a boy or girl pairing off from a party for a 'kiss and cuddle'

barry - good fun, brilliant - as in 'that's a barrie record'

bogle - (see sneg/snotter)

boot - an ugly woman: as in 'yer ma's an old boot'

chore/chorie - steal, purloin (with humorous admiration) as in 'I chorred it from the supermarket'

chum - as in 'Go on and chum me' ('Please accompany me')

divi - stupid ('Yon's a real divi)

doon the street - to walk to the main street (usually for shopping). Also 'I'll get ye doon the street' ('I'll accompany you')

gadge/gadgie - a man, guy ('See that gadgie over there?)

geggie - face ('Shut yer geggie')

gob - spittal or to spit (also mouth as in 'shut yer gob')

hack/hackit - ugly and mean-minded as in 'that's a hackit old bitch'

mince - rubbish ('That video's mince!')

morte - a woman ('I was out wi ma morte the ither night')

nash - to hurry, rush ('Come on, let's nash home')

pagger - kick in, batter ('We're gonna pagger him the night')

puss - face: ('I gave him a smack right in the puss')

radge - an idiot, madman ('That guy's a real radge')

scud - hit ('I gave him a real scud on the puss')

scran - food ('I Love ma scran')

scranner - a beggar, scrounger ('That's a real scranner')

shan - frightening, rotten, horrible, sneaky ('It was shan what he did)

shotty! - watch out!

skegs - pants slag - 'take the mickey'

sneg/snotter - 'green slimey thing that comes down yer nose'

treg - a tramp ('He came doon the street dressed like an old treg')

Appendix C
Edinburgh LOWLAND SCOTS

Ashet - pottery dish
Bairn - a child
Blether - chatter, gossip
Brae - hill
Breeks - trousers
Buroo - Labour Exchange (Job Centre)
Cuddy - donkey
Dither - in a state of indecision
Dyke - stone wall
Doo - pigeon (tame)
Douce - gentle, sedate
Fly - sly
Haar - mist (from the sea)
Keelie - guttersnipe, urchin
Kirk - church
Licht - light
Lug - ear
Oxter - armpit
Peenie - pinafore
Press - wall cupboard
Sclater - woodlouse
Scunner - disgust
Sudger - soldier
Sybo/Sybies - shallot
Wabbit - tired out
Tattie - potato
Wee - small, little

INDEX of NAMES